THE BEST OF ENGLAND

THE BEST OF

ENGLAND

Illustrated throughout in color

GARRY HOGG

ARCO PUBLISHING COMPANY, INC.
New York

Published in 1974 by Arco Publishing Company, Inc.
219 Park Avenue South, New York, N.Y. 10003

Library of Congress Catalog Card Number 74–75396

ISBN 0–668–03455–6

Printed in Great Britain

CONTENTS

DEDICATION

I dedicate this edition of my book to those many Americans whom I have come to know through correspondence resulting from their reading earlier books of mine about England. Especially to those who have, on their visits in search of The Best of England, taken the trouble to call me or, better still, come to visit me at my home, often bearing with them copies of some book of mine bought in the United States but brought with them to serve as itinerary-guides while touring here. Such correspondence, such encounters, are true bonuses in the lives of writers of travel and topographical books who have sought to communicate their own enthusiasm to their potential readers. I hope that this new book will serve to remind visitors who already know England of what they have already seen, and also persuade those who have not yet been here to come and see for themselves what one writer at least regards as The Best of England.

GARRY HOGG

Groombridge,
Kent, England

LONDON

BUCKINGHAM PALACE

The slightly irreverent name, 'Buck House', derives from the fact that the original building belonged to the Duke of Buckingham, from whom George III bought it in 1762. On ascending the throne, his son, George IV, called in the famous architect, John Nash, to remodel it in 1825. Nash's Marble Arch was originally designed as the main entrance to it. George IV named it his palace but, strangely, never occupied it; the first monarch to do so was Victoria, and during and since her day it has been the reigning sovereign's London residence. Edward VII was born and also died there.

The East Wing, facing St James's Park, was added in 1847; in 1913 the whole east façade was redesigned in the more dignified style which confronts us today. The interior is not open to the public and it is only from photographs that we glean some notion of the splendour of, for example, the 66-foot long Throne Room. The royal apartments are situated generally in the North Wing. The Queen's Private Chapel, in the South Wing, was badly damaged during World War Two and had largely to be rebuilt. The opportunity was taken, in 1961, to adapt part of this in such a way as to form the Queen's Gallery. This is open to the public, and in it may be seen one of the most outstanding private collections of art treasures existing anywhere in the world.

The main façade is the work of the architect Sir Aston Webb, and it is from the balcony midway along its great length that the sovereign permits herself to be seen on occasions of public rejoicing. But this is not the true 'front' of the palace at all. The true front overlooks the forty acres of garden not accessible to the public, the setting for the occasional Royal Garden Parties to which the elect in various walks of life are specially invited – the invitations being highly prized. In the gardens may be found a mulberry tree, originally planted by James I in 1609 in an attempt to encourage the silk industry in England. The so-called Mulberry Gardens fell into disrepute in the seventeenth century and were condemned by Samuel Pepys. South of the palace may be found the Royal Mews, which are open on certain days to the general public. Here may be seen the sovereign's horses and carriages, and most notably the State Coach, designed in 1762 – the year in which the Duke of Buckingham sold out to George III.

HOUSES OF PARLIAMENT

Its true name is the 'New Palace of Westminster', for it occupies the site of an ancient palace which, from the reign of Edward the Confessor, nine centuries ago, to that of Henry VIII, was the sovereign's London residence. Old Palace Yard was formerly an inner court of the palace, and until 1800 the House of Lords assembled in a chamber at the south end which was the scene of the famous Gunpowder Plot in 1605.

The vast building covers some eight acres on a riverside site almost 1,000 feet long. The Upper House (of Lords) is an elaborately ornate chamber 90 feet long by 45 feet high and wide; it contains the thrones of the sovereign and escort – the latter being one inch lower than the former. The Lower House – or House of Commons – is to the north of the Central Hall, a chamber 130 feet long, 43 feet high and 48 feet wide. Almost completely destroyed in 1941, it was lovingly rebuilt; today it is entered through the Churchill Arch, constructed of stone salvaged from the bombing and fire. The Speaker's Chair came from Australia, and the Table of the House, on which the Mace lies when Parliament is sitting, came from the Dominion of Canada.

Historically and aesthetically, the most famous, and certainly the largest of this vast complex of chambers is Westminster Hall, 290 feet long, 92 feet high and 68 feet wide. It dates from 1399, when it replaced the original chamber built in 1097. Here, in 1649, Charles I heard himself condemned to execution: a brass tablet on the steps on which he sat commemorates the occasion. Here, in 1327, Edward II abdicated. And here too, ironically, Richard II, who built the hall, with its superb roof, was deposed from his unhappy throne.

Most of the building was destroyed by fire in 1834; it was immediately rebuilt by Sir Charles Barry in neo-Gothic style. It contains the crypt of St Stephens, and the cloisters; eleven courtyards, 100 staircases, two miles of corridors and over 1,000 apartments. The Victoria Tower, 336 feet high and 75 feet square, is the loftiest square tower in the world; the Central Spire is 300 feet high; the Clock Tower, 320 feet high, contains Big Ben, whose four dials are 23 feet square and minute hands 14 feet long. The Union Jack flies from the Victoria Tower by day and a light burns in the Clock Tower by night at all times when Parliament is in session.

PICCADILLY CIRCUS

Still popularly, if unjustifiably these days, referred to as 'the hub of the British Empire', this remains for most Londoners and visitors alike the focal point of the metropolis. Streets radiating from it are, notably, Piccadilly to the south-west, bordered by Green Park, arrow-straight towards Buckingham Palace; and, northwards, Regent Street and Shaftesbury Avenue, named after the 7th Earl of Shaftesbury, friend of the deprived. Tribute was paid to him by the erection of the misnamed Eros, a pyramidal bronze fountain topped by the dainty figure of the Angel of Christian Charity, the first monument in England to have been sculptured in aluminium. It was unveiled in 1893, eight years after the philanthropic earl's death. The £3,000 which Sir Alfred Gilbert received for his masterpiece was regarded by him as so inadequate that he was roused to fury and shook off the dust of England from his feet for ever! A number of schemes for the redesigning of the Circus have been proposed; a time must soon come when it will be completely altered and, it is to be fervently hoped, its garish display of vast advertisements removed once and for all.

GROSVENOR SQUARE

This is popularly known as 'Little America', for it is almost wholly surrounded by United States administrative buildings. The whole west side is occupied by the vast embassy, designed by Eero Saarinen in 1958. As long ago as 1785, John Adams, American Ambassador and later President, lived at No. 9, and so instituted the link. But its history is older than that. It was laid out by Sir Richard Grosvenor in 1695 on a site fortified by Londoners fifty years earlier at the start of the Civil War. Lord Chesterfield occupied No. 43 in the mid-eighteenth century; before him, the house had been occupied by the Duchess of Kendall, mistress to George I. At No. 24, the Earl of Shaftesbury lived for a time, and at No. 17, Admiral Lord Beatty, of World War One naval fame, died in 1936; both these houses are now demolished.

The elegant and spacious Square was laid out by the great landscape gardener, William Kent. It is overlooked from its north side by a fine statue of President Franklin D. Roosevelt, sculptured by Sir W. Reid Dick. This, with Saarinen's American Embassy, serves as a reminder that this is not so much London as 'Little America'.

ST PAUL'S CATHEDRAL

This is, essentially, the City of London's church. Traditionally, a Roman temple to Diana stood on the site at the top of Ludgate Hill; there was a Christian church here in Saxon times, burned down, rebuilt, and burned down again in 1087. It was immediately rebuilt, and progressively extended until, in the Middle Ages, 'Old St Paul's' was the longest cathedral in England, 600 feet, with a 460-foot steeple that was destroyed by lightning in 1561. Fire has been a repeated menace right up to the bombing in 1941. In 1666 the cathedral was almost totally destroyed in the Great Fire that succeeded the Great Plague. Rebuilding to Sir Christopher Wren's designs began in 1675 and was completed in 1710. A smoke-blackened stone from the burned-out cathedral, bearing the inscription *RESURGAM* – 'I shall rise again' – was incorporated by him in his new building, his supreme masterpiece: a symbol with a significance.

His Renaissance-style edifice is vast: 515 feet long, 227 feet across its transepts, its west-front towers 212 feet high, with 17-ton 'Great Paul' and the clock in the south-west one. The most remarkable feature is of course the dome, 112 feet in diameter, carrying the lantern and gilded cross to a height of 365 feet. If St Paul's were to be placed on the bed of the North Sea, lantern and cross would still be seen. The interior of the dome is 218 feet above the floor; to obtain the best view of the cathedral as a whole, it should be viewed from beneath this.

Monuments and memorials to the great in many walks of life and many ages meet the eye on every side. At the end of the south choir aisle is the figure of John Donne, seventeenth-century poet and Dean of St Paul's, still bearing marks of the fire that destroyed Old St Paul's; he alone survived. In the south aisle is the 'prelates' throne', a memorial to the first Australian peer; close by is Holman Hunt's famous painting, 'The Light of the World'. The Jesus Chapel, in the apse, is the memorial to the 28,000 Americans who fell in World War Two. The north transept was the part of the cathedral most badly damaged in that war by enemy bombs; much of it collapsed into the crypt, where you will find Wren's own tomb, the giant sarcophagus containing the remains of the Duke of Wellington, and another containing those of Nelson, in a coffin made from the mainmast of a French ship defeated by him at Trafalgar. The history enshrined in this magnificent setting is endless, the names immortal.

THE TOWER OF LONDON

The finest view of this 'saga in stone' is undoubtedly that obtained from the South Bank. The term is appropriate, for this huge castle incorporates nearly twenty centuries of history. There may still be seen relics of the fortress built by the Romans at this river crossing now spanned by the enormous bascules of Tower Bridge. Centuries later, King Alfred reinforced it. Centuries later still, William the Conqueror made use of what he found to enclose the fortress he designed to ward-off potential invaders from the east. An outer curtain wall, a moat, and an inner curtain wall made the site virtually impregnable. Within these, he threw up the huge keep, the essential feature of all Norman castles, known for nine centuries past as the White Tower. Its 15-foot thick walls, 100 feet long on each side, rise to 90 feet in height, forming one of the largest as well as the earliest of all keeps built in Europe.

Massively constructed as they are, the towers and bastions – Bloody Tower, Beauchamp, Martin, Byward, Salt and Wakefield among them – seem dwarfed by it into insignificance. In these have languished kings and queens – among them Anne Boleyn and Katharine Howard, two of Henry VIII's unhappy wives who, like so many others, passed through the ill-omened Traitor's Gate. The tally of assassins and would-be assassins such as the Dukes of Buckingham and Monmouth and the Earl of Essex, and Guy Fawkes who in 1605 sought to blow up the Houses of Parliament, is seemingly endless; so too is that of men and women, innocent as well as guilty, whose execution took place within these grim, forbidding walls.

Within these walls, too, is the Weapon Room and, another engrossing section of the Armoury, the Sword Room. The Martin Tower was the setting only three hundred or so years ago for the abortive attempt by one Colonel Blood to steal the Crown Jewels, placed there for safety. Beneath the Great Tower is a staircase site beneath which, again about three centuries ago, two broken skeletons were discovered, to be identified as those of Edward V and his younger brother and thus clear up a mystery that has been linked for five centuries past with Richard III, who was killed by the Earl of Richmond's rebel army at the Battle of Bosworth Field in 1485. History and drama confront you at every turn within these encircling walls.

TRAFALGAR SQUARE

This is the original site of the Royal Mews, now behind Buckingham Palace. It was laid out between 1829 and 1841 and described by Sir Robert Peel as 'the finest site in Europe'. It has increasingly become the focal point for gatherings and demonstrations of many kinds. Here, every year, a christmas tree, presented to the people of London by the people of Norway, is ceremonially illuminated; each tree is, by tradition, a foot higher than its predecessor. Dominating the Square is the 167-foot fluted granite column carrying the 18-foot statue of Admiral Lord Nelson, victor at the Battle of Trafalgar in 1805. The four bronze lions, *couchant*, were modelled by Landseer, and the four bronze reliefs on the plinth were cast from cannon taken from the defeated French men-o'-war.

More beautiful, if less impressive, are the fountains rising above the crowds that fill the square day and night. The equestrian statue at the north-east corner is of George IV; in the long north parapet are commemorative busts of Lords Jellicoe and Beatty, of World War One naval fame. Over-looking them is the National Gallery, whose fine Corinthian columns were taken from a palace built for the Prince Regent; just behind it, opposite the statue of Nurse Edith Cavell, shot by the Germans in World War One, is the National Portrait Gallery. On the west side is Canada House and on the east side is South Africa House. On the north-east corner stands the church of St Martin-in-the-Fields, regarded as the finest creation of the eighteenth-century architect James Gibbs but occupying the site of a much older church. It has a richly decorative ceiling, the work of Artari and Bagutti, and a font dating from 1689. In the famous crypt, formerly a burial-vault, there is the ancient parish chest and, a small feature all too often overlooked, the parish whipping-post. The crypt has long been an overnight place of shelter for London's down-and-outs. On the diametrically opposite corner of Trafalgar Square stands the imposing Admiralty Arch, giving access to The Mall and St James's Park beyond. Close by is the upper end of Whitehall, lined by important Government Offices, offering the best view of Nelson's Column. Midway down its length is Horse Guards' Parade; after that, the Cenotaph and Downing Street, culminating in Parliament Square and the Houses of Parliament.

WESTMINSTER ABBEY

According to tradition, the 'Collegiate Church of St Peter in Westminster' stands on a site once known as Thorney Isle on which a Saxon church was consecrated in AD 616. The first authenticated record of a church here is that of a Benedictine Abbey established in AD 730; it was named 'Western Monastery' (or Minster) because it stood to the west of the City of London. Edward the Confessor, the monk-king who died in 1066, rebuilt the abbey on a much larger scale, and his remains were subsequently laid here to rest. Here too lie buried Henry III, Henry VII, Elizabeth I, Charles II, William III, Queen Anne and George II; and here too every British sovereign has been crowned, with the exception of Edward V and Edward VIII, since King Harold.

The abbey is regarded as probably the finest example we have of Early English architecture – save for the Perpendicular chapel at the east end, built by Henry VII, and the eighteenth-century twin towers at the west end. It is to Henry III that we owe the greater part of the glorious building we see today. It is 513 feet long and 200 feet wide across the transepts and possesses the loftiest Gothic nave in England, 102 feet in height. Just inside the west door is the tomb of the Unknown Warrior of World War I, brought here to represent 'the bravely dumb that did their deed, and scorned to blot it with a name'; he lies in earth brought from the battlefields of Flanders. The south-west tower soaring above his tomb contains the Chapel of St George, dedicated to the memory of those who died in two world wars; outside it is a plaque to the memory of President F. D. Roosevelt.

The Chapel of Henry VII, with its glorious fan-tracery vaulting, is a superb example of Tudor-Gothic. In the Chapel of Edward the Confessor is the Coronation Chair which encloses the famous 'Stone of Scone' carried away from Scotland by Edward I in 1297 and used for all subsequent coronations. Poets' Corner (named after Chaucer and Spenser) contains tombs, plaques and memorials to a host of names: Tennyson and Browning, Dryden and Blake, Milton, Wordsworth and Coleridge, Shakespeare, Burns and Keats, Ben Jonson, the Brontës and countless others. Other memorials commemorate Livingstone, Wesley, Isaac Newton, the American philanthropist George Peabody and hundreds more. Westminster Abbey is indeed history enshrined in ancient stone.

STATELY HOMES AND CASTLES

Sussex

ARUNDEL CASTLE

This is as good an example as any you could find of the old saying that 'an Englishman's home is his castle'. For not only is this one of the finest and most famous castles in the country, it is also the country seat of England's premier earl, the Duke of Norfolk, latest in the long line of the Howard Family that dates back to Elizabethan times. It stands high on a wooded eminence dominating the charming little Sussex town of Arundel and is seen most effectively from the south side of the gently flowing river at the foot of the slope, its chimneys standing out above its battlemented walls. From this viewpoint it suggests Great House rather than Castle (save for one massive tower); but once you have passed through the thirteenth-century barbican and climbed the turf slope and steps to the great circular keep, with its 10-foot thick walls, you are aware of it as Castle rather than Great House any more, though it is in fact a classic combination of the two.

There is believed to have been a castle on this site as far back as the days of King Alfred, but the one there today, as for the past nine centuries, like all our most imposing castles is of Norman design and construction. It possesses a double bailey – that characteristic enclosed courtyard, known also as a ward, in which the tournaments were often held. Look out for the magnificent inner gateway, built by Roger Montgomery four years after the Battle of Hastings, at which he fought so valiantly alongside William the Conqueror: constructed of local flint and stone, it is as intact today, after all those centuries, as the day the masons completed it. You can climb on to the battlements from which, according to tradition, the feudal Warden of the Castle hurled his sword, Mongley, down the long slope of the park, crying out that he would be buried where it fell.

As might be expected, the interior of much of Arundel Castle rings with a martial rather than a domestic note, even though this is both home and residence. There is a warlike 'feel' in the huge Barons' Hall, and even in the more domestic rooms. But what lingers in the memory after one has left is the vast assembly of round towers, curtain-walls, battlements, dungeons and vaults and massive façades on which the imprint of cannon-balls can still be detected, vivid reminders of a stormy past that has melted, nine hundred years later, into massive serenity.

Hampshire

BEAULIEU ABBEY
(Off B 3054, 10 miles S. of Southampton)

On the edge of the attractive small village of Beaulieu, situated on the west bank of the river of the same name (translated, it could hardly be more apt), is the ancestral home of Lord Montagu. Founded in AD 1204 by King John for monks of the Cistercian Order, it survived until the Dissolution, when, unhappily, much of the stonework was removed for use at Hurst Castle and elsewhere. But the fourteenth-century Outer Gate House survives and is today part of the Palace House in which Lord Montagu lives.

The huge area formerly covered by the abbey church and cloister, chapter house, dormitory, refectory, kitchen, guest-house, infirmary and so forth has been skilfully turned to modern uses; or, where only vestiges remain, marked out in such a way that the medieval abbey comes forcefully to life. Among the uses to which they have been put is, most notably, that supreme attraction, the National Motor Museum. This was founded by the owner in 1952 and thanks to his enthusiasm has developed into the premier museum of its kind in the world. It has outgrown its original space, and now occupies an area of some 70,000 square feet, the 300 and more exhibits illustrating the whole story of the motor car from its birth in the nineteenth century onwards.

Abbey, Palace, Museum: you may visit this complex of buildings old and not-so-old and satisfy a range of interests. As a ruined abbey partly restored it reveals how dedicated men lived their lives seven centuries ago. As a Great House it offers a wealth of beauty and treasure amassed by generations of owners. The Picture Gallery, for instance, has a notable display of masterpieces by great artists; the Inner Hall of the Great Gate House has a superb thirteenth-century fan-vaulted ceiling; the Upper Drawing Room, converted from the South Chapel over the Great Gate House, has in one of its walls the medieval piscina and aumbry: the secular and the sacred in close association. There are other such examples at Beaulieu, and this co-ordination of ages and uses in building and furnishing is not only unusual but hauntingly memorable. Add to this *mélange* of abbey and palace the exhibits in the Motor Museum and it will be seen that there is something memorable here for most tastes; and in a rural setting that must appeal powerfully to every lover of the natural scene.

24

Gloucestershire

BERKELEY CASTLE
(Just W. of A 38, and M 5, midway between Bristol and Gloucester)

Most of what confronts the visitor today is of thirteenth- and fourteenth-century origin, but inside the vast encircling walls, fourteen feet thick and massively buttressed, there are relics of its Norman origin, notably the great keep which was built to the command of Henry II for the Fitzhardings, who became the Earls of Berkeley and live there to this day. It is among the most ancient of England's Great Houses and has been continuously occupied by the same family for the whole of its long life.

Beautifully situated on the east side of the Severn, it commands a magnificent panorama westwards over the Welsh border. In such a setting, it is difficult to credit that it was the scene of deliberate and evil murder. Within its complex of ramparted walls, turrets, octagonal towers, sinister archways and dungeons carved out beneath the towers, there took place in 1327 the fearful murder of King Edward II at the instigation of his queen and with the collaboration of the Earl of Mortimer. The gruesomeness of the circumstances of this foul deed, one that stood out even in an age when such murders were commonplace, has lent an aura of evil that indeed haunts much of the interior of the castle even to this day, despite its romantic setting in pastureland dotted by stands of noble trees, the terraced walks of velvety turf and the expanses of calm water in which the grandeur of the castle is reflected.

Among the most imposing rooms is the Great Hall, sixty feet in length and broad in proportion. In rooms such as this and in the linking corridors are to be found the treasures that have been accumulated during the eight centuries that the Earls of Berkeley have occupied their home. Beneath the fine vaulted ceilings stand pieces of furniture that are priceless; on the panelled walls hang not only splendid tapestries, but in addition to rare portraits, trophies such as you rightly expect to find in the possession of such a family as this. Also to be seen is the world-famous collection of Berkeley Silver; and, perhaps even more fittingly, a magnificent display of arms and armour. Here, then, is everything the visitor could look for in such a setting, whether his interest is that of a specialist in medieval history and architecture or that of a lover of fine craftsmanship and artists' masterpieces.

Oxfordshire

BLENHEIM PALACE

In August 1704, John Churchill, 1st Duke of Marlborough, crushingly defeated King Louis XIV's army at Blenheim and thus effectively thwarted that monarch's ambitions. Queen Anne resolved that he must be suitably rewarded, and conferred the Royal Manor of Woodstock on the duke and his heirs 'in perpetuity'. Her Parliament donated £240,000 – a staggering sum in those days, though every last penny of it was to be needed; the great architect of the day, Sir John Vanbrugh, was called in; Blenheim Palace was the result. It took seventeen years to build. On 30 November 1874, in a small room on the ground floor to the west of the Great Hall, a descendant of the 1st Duke, Sir Winston Churchill, first saw the light. At his own request he lies, not in Westminster Abbey but in the churchyard of the tiny church of Bladon, hardly more than a stone's throw distant from this vast palace which covers no less than seven acres of the 2,500 acres of parkland that surround it.

Palace is the appropriate word for this magnificently conceived country house; everything about it is on the heroic scale. The Long Library, with its ornate ceiling, is 180 feet in length, dwarfing even the great organ that occupies one end. The Great Hall is almost seventy feet high to the Thornhill ceiling that depicts vividly the Battle of Blenheim; it has stone ornamentation 'Cutt Extrordingry Rich and Sunk Very Deep' by that great wood- and stone-carver, Grinling Gibbons. So massively constructed is this palatial edifice that stone had to be brought from no fewer than twenty quarries, a whole army of men and horses being employed in its transport. The wealth of treasures in the countless vast rooms – tapestries, paintings, sculptures, furniture, murals, trophies, the famous Rysbrack Tomb in the Chapel – can hardly be surpassed in any other of England's Great Houses.

'Capability' Brown laid out avenues to represent the field of Blenheim. The Triumphal Way is world-famous; the Sunken Italian Gardens no less; the Water Gardens are reminiscent of those at the Palace of Versailles. Blenheim was designed not only as a reward for services rendered to a country but as something of a National Monument in itself. It was built for one great warrior; it is perhaps even better known today as the birthplace of his descendant, himself a great warrior, the late Sir Winston Churchill.

CASTLE HOWARD
(Off A 64 York–Malton road, 6 miles W. of Malton)

This is one of the finest Stately Homes in a county exceptionally rich in such possessions, and indeed in all England. Palace would be more appropriate as a name for it than castle. In fact, Horace Walpole, no mean judge of great houses, wrote of it: 'I have seen gigantic palaces before, but never such a sublime one.' He did not exaggerate. It reminds the visitor of Blenheim Palace; and this is hardly surprising, for the architect of both was Sir John Vanbrugh. Blenheim took seventeen years to build; Castle Howard took thirty-seven; the architect and, incidentally, the 3rd Earl of Carlisle who commissioned Vanbrugh to build it, were both dead before the last touches were put to the enormous pile in 1737.

Everything about Castle Howard was designed and executed on the heroic scale that was to be repeated at Blenheim. Even to approach it you must pass along a seemingly endless drive, through beautiful parkland extending to more than 1,000 acres and dominated by a 100-foot high obelisk erected midway through the decades during which the project was taking shape. Vanbrugh designed the huge entrance beneath a magnificent cupola, a feature unknown at that time in private dwellings however ambitious. His immense frontage extends on either side of this, with ornate arched windows, elaborate friezes, pilasters topped by large urns and even more imposing statues, to merge into two enormous yet well proportioned wings. From this entrance you pass into the marble entrance hall that is wholly in keeping with the grandeur of the exterior. Thereafter it is a sequence of magnificent rooms: the Long Gallery; the Orleans Room with its famous collection of Zuccarellis; the Octagon Room with its even more famous, indeed priceless, Holbeins; the Corridor with its collection of Pre-Raphaelites; the Tapestry Room with its superb collection on display, and so on.

The grounds are hardly less memorable. In addition to the dominating Obelisk there is the Temple of the Four Winds; the Doric Mausoleum, as large as one of Wren's smaller churches; the Satyr Gate; the Great Fountain, with its giant Atlas supporting on his massive shoulders an enormous globe. Unlike many Stately Homes, this one is occupied by its owners, whose name it bears; for all its vastness, therefore, it gives the sense of being lived in and is thus more truly a home than a museum piece.

Kent

CHARTWELL MANOR
(3 miles S-E. of Westerham, 5 miles W. of Sevenoaks)

This is a 'Great House' not because of its size or splendour – like Blenheim, Woburn, Castle Howard, Chatsworth or Knole; its claim to greatness lies essentially in its associations, since 1922 when he bought it, with Sir Winston Churchill. From that date until his death more than forty years later, this was his beloved country home. It is now National Trust property, and so will be fittingly preserved for all time.

More than ever Blenheim, his birthplace, could be, this small manor house, largely Victorian though with later additions, is imbued with the presence of Churchill; to enter it is to come immediately into contact with it – very much alive. On the walls are many of the pictures he painted: one of the two almost obsessive hobbies that doubtless enabled him to achieve some peace of mind amid the hurly-burly in which for most of his long lifetime he contrived to involve himself. (The other hobby, not strange in view of his creative flair and abundant energy, was wall-building; specimens of his brick-laying are abundant in the garden, notably the cottage he built for his daughter.)

Appropriately, some of the rooms have been left set out exactly as they were when he moved about among them, though others have been made museum-like. You will see the famous working-desk at which so much of his matchless prose was written: a gift from his children, it remains as he left it the last time he got up from his chair. The much larger writing-desk, standing on a superb Tehran carpet that was a gift from the Shah of Persia on his 69th birthday, was formerly Lord Randolph Churchill's. An eighteenth-century spinet has been adapted to display his collection of medallions. In the Library there is a model of the famous 'Mulberry Harbour' used on 'D-Day-plus-109', 23 September 1944, a reminder (if such were needed) that Churchill's inspiration lay behind this brilliant conception, as it did behind so much else. One ironic exhibit, in view of de Gaulle's love–hate relationship with Britain, is a beautiful Lalique glass cock, emblem of France, presented to Lady Churchill by the General himself. Wren's epitaph reads: '*Si monumentum requiris, circumspice*'; the words could be used equally here at Chartwell, for the very air is redolent of the great man for whom it was a treasured country retreat for so many wearying years.

PORT ARROMANCHES.
D+109

LEGEND

Middlesex

HAMPTON COURT PALACE

This former royal palace was built for himself by Cardinal Wolsey, Lord Chancellor of England, designed to be the finest private residence in England. In a desperate attempt to regain the favour of his unpredictable monarch, he presented it to Henry VIII almost before he himself had lived in it. The king took it for granted, and added the Chapel and the Great Hall. For two hundred years it was a Royal Residence. Edward VI was born there; five of Henry's six queens were installed there; Mary and Elizabeth I held court there; Charles I lived there both as king and as condemned prisoner. Successive monarchs altered, added to and enriched the original fabric. But George III took an unaccountable dislike to the place, and from his day onwards, though still called a palace, it has been not a residence but a superb show-piece housing a royal museum of unparalleled splendour. It may be that George III felt it to be haunted by the cardinal's unhappy ghost, or by that of William III, who died after being thrown from his saddle while riding in its glorious parkland.

What confronts you today is largely the work of Sir Christopher Wren: a noble yet mellow exterior housing an interior of monumental and moving splendour, redolent of the treasured possessions of a succession of monarchs. Exterior features such as the Great Gatehouse, the Moat Bridge, the Base Court, Fountain Court and Anne Boleyn's Gateway, the second gate tower, command admiration by their immediate impact. Within, you progress from one great chamber to another, with a heightening sense of what is meant by the term palatial. In the King's Guard Chamber there is a magnificent display of no fewer than 3,000 individual pieces of weaponry; among the innumerable fine tapestries are those from Flanders on the walls of the Great Watching Chamber, from which persons granted audience of the reigning monarch passed into the Presence Chamber; among the many notable ceilings, including the finest Renaissance ceiling in the country, are those of Wolsey's Closet, the Queen's Drawing Room, William III's State Bedroom and the King's Staircase, with its glorious balustrade by that craftsman in wrought iron, Jean Tijou. Indeed, the treasures are inexhaustible; so, after surfeit, it is a relief to be able to walk in the beautifully and lavishly filled gardens that form the perfect setting for this building of mellow brick and fine stone.

RABY CASTLE
(On A 688, 1 mile N. of Staindrop)

Even Alnwick Castle, across the border in Northumberland, hardly rivals this Great House in its immediate impact: this is obviously a fortified residence rather than just a gracious country seat of some landowner. Even from a distance, it is impressive to the point of formidability; that impression is strengthened as you pass through the Great Gateway into the court-yard amid a complex of no fewer than nine enormous towers linked by walls. In the twelfth century this was the stronghold of the great clan of the Nevills, and that gateway is still referred to as Nevills' Tower. No two of these nine towers are the same. In height to their turrets and battlements they range from the 60 feet of Joan's Tower to the 80 feet of Clifford's Tower; others of hardly less imposing stature include the Watch Tower, the Raskelf, Bulmer and Keep Towers. The first stones were laid as early as 1016 – half a century before the Norman Conquest; but what confronts the visitor today is largely of the fourteenth century. Seen from the far side of the encircling moat, it looks impregnable.

The interior is hardly less impressive. In the vast Barons' Hall, on 13 November (ominous date) 1569 the historic Rising of the North, designed to replace Elizabeth I on the throne by Mary, was planned. The failure of the conspiracy led to the temporary forfeiture of Raby Castle to the Crown. The 40-foot high kitchen is little changed from the layout of six centuries ago. The dining-room is especially notable for the beautiful chimney-piece of snow-white marble. The Octagon Room has a lofty vaulted ceiling and walls covered with yellow silk panels. The entrance, known as the Lower Hall, is particularly memorable: its great length is emphasised by a double row, or 'avenue', of octagonal pillars lining a 'carriageway' laid down in the eighteenth century in honour of a returning scion of the family.

The stronghold-like 'feel' of the exterior and interior has been softened by the display of treasures, such as the famous collection of statues and the portraits by such artists as Kneller, Lely and Sir Joshua Reynolds. The blend of the romantic and the grim is somehow epitomised in the beautifully named Rose of Raby Room, which is actually situated in the great keep itself.

Berkshire

WINDSOR CASTLE
(On A 308, 23 miles W. of London)

To its citizens this is a town of some 30,000 inhabitants pleasantly sited on the south bank of the Thames twenty-odd miles up-river from London. Parts of their Guildhall are attributed to Sir Christopher Wren; among the many seventeenth-century houses is one formerly occupied by Nell Gwynne; there are many charming eighteenth-century houses, gracious and serene; Church Street is particularly memorable for its smaller buildings. The High Street, where you will find the Church of St John, with its Grinling Gibbons railings and de Cleyn's painting of the Last Supper, a gift from George III, dips steeply to the bridge that carries the road across the river to Eton College. The vast Windsor Great Park, more than 2,000 acres in extent, part-circles this royal town to the east and south; it is a much-visited Nature Reserve.

To the visitor, whether from overseas or not, Windsor is, quite simply: The Castle. Smaller than Sandringham, Balmoral or Buckingham Palace, it is by far the most spectacular of all our monarchs' residences; it has served as such for the nine hundred-odd years of its existence. It not only dominates the town of Windsor and the wide river flowing at its feet (from the north bank of which it presents its most impressive aspect), but is the largest inhabited castle in the world.

William the Conqueror picked this strategic site and built the first, timber, fortress on it. Thereafter, a long succession of monarchs set their architects, engineers and masons to work on it. Timber was replaced by stonework; Henry II built its most imposing feature, the great keep commonly known as the Round Tower, the hub of the whole massive complex; from its turret the Royal Standard flies to indicate that the reigning monarch is in residence. Henry III constructed the enormous walls that, with their hard verticals and castellations, contrast so effectively with the massive circle of the keep. Edward III was born here, and here founded the Order of the Knights of the Garter. You pass through Henry VIII's Gateway, with its polygonal flanking towers, into St George's Chapel, the dominating feature of the Lower Ward; thence to the Middle Ward, dominated by the Round Tower; and so to the Upper Ward, where the State Apartments may be visited. Nine centuries of history lie about you.

Bedfordshire

WOBURN ABBEY
(In Woburn, on A 50, 8 miles N–W. of Dunstable)

This Stately Home has been termed 'the most truly English of all'. It is by no means the oldest, for the enormous building you see today dates from the eighteenth and very early nineteenth centuries. But it has been the home of the Dukes of Bedford for three centuries (there is an unbroken sequence of their portraits on the walls) and, more important, has been consistently occupied by successive generations to this day. The exterior may strike the visitor as somewhat austere; the treasures inside, not to be matched in any other Great House in the land, will leave him breathless with wonder.

Among the fourteen State Rooms there is the State Bedroom, where monarchs from Charles I to Victoria have slept. The State Saloon possesses a most remarkable domed ceiling. The State Dining Room is laid out with gold plate and silver-gilt cutlery and a magnificent Sèvres dinner service, overlooked by paintings by Van Dyck. Perhaps the most famous room of all is the Canaletto Room, on whose walls hang no fewer than twenty-one masterpieces by that great artist of the Venetian scene. The value of the art treasures at Woburn alone runs into many millions of pounds; one Rembrandt has been valued at £750,000, and the Sèvres dinner service, a gift to the 4th Duke's wife from Louis XV, consists of nearly 200 pieces. The Chippendale, Sheraton, European and Chinese furniture, the paintings by Velasquez, Frans Hals, Murillo, Gainsborough, Poussin and a score of other famous artists, the tapestries and murals and sculptures, the porcelain and glass: the tally of rare treasures accumulated by generations of the family within these walls is seemingly endless.

Nor do the marvellous resources of Woburn lie solely within its walls. The house stands amid 3,000 acres of parkland. Here, notably in the now world-famous Safari Park, are to be found animals, some of them quite unique in this country, others to be seen only in the larger zoos. Here, roaming at liberty, are American bison, Australian wallabies, Soay sheep, Formosan Sika and Manchurian deer, sarus, cranes, rheas and the quite unique Père David deer, from the former Imperial Hunting Lodge at Peking; such specimens as are to be found elsewhere in the world were all bred from the unique Woburn herd. This parkland is the living counterpart of the man-made treasures that abound within the stately chambers of this Great House.

CATHEDRALS AND CITIES

Somerset

BATH

It has been said that 'the reason for the existence of Bath is – water'. The clue lies in the city's ancient name, *Aquae Sulis*, given to it by the Romans who discovered the healing properties of the mineral waters which still, as was the case some 2,000 years ago, gush from the hot springs at the rate of a quarter of a million gallons a day. For the Romans, this was the finest spa in the country they invaded; it remains so still, though the actual baths they constructed vanished after their departure and were not discovered until less than a century ago, in 1879. The mineral springs, however, were known in medieval days; they reached their apotheosis in the eighteenth century when England's élite converged upon Bath to 'take the waters'; and they are in active use to this day. Bath is, essentially, however, an eighteenth-century city; Richard 'Beau' Nash set his seal on it in that century and became 'King of Bath'; its tradition of elegance and gentility (perhaps a despised term today?) derives largely from his influence and that of his close associates.

Architecturally, this is the most perfectly integrated of English cities. Almost all its buildings, large and small, are of the lovely 'Bath' stone, the hue and texture of which, apart from the design and use, give a glowing quality to the city that haunts the memory. Among its outstanding features may be named in particular Robert Adam's Pulteney Bridge, strongly reminiscent of the Ponte Vecchio in Florence; the Assembly Rooms, also dating from the end of the eighteenth century, which incidentally house one of the most notable collections of period costumes in Europe; the superbly designed Royal Crescent, a part-ellipse of thirty elegant houses overlooking a curved slope of fine turf; Pulteney Street itself, considered by many connoisseurs to be the finest street in Europe – though natives of Edinburgh might challenge this; and of course the famous eighteenth-century Pump Room, focal point of the city, and the much older Abbey, skilfully restored in the same lovely stone as the original after the Dissolution.

Two miles from the city centre is Claverton Manor, housing the American Museum in Britain; here two centuries of American domestic life may be leisurely surveyed on the outskirts of a city whose own history dates back two thousand years and more.

CAMBRIDGE

There is only one other English city that can match this for the all-pervading sense of 'history in stone' it imparts: Oxford. The debate as to which university city is the more beautiful can never be resolved; that as to which is the older has been resolved historically to the satisfaction of Oxonians, but the margin between them is small. Oldest of European universities is the Sorbonne; those of Oxford and Cambridge derive from Paris refugee students who sought asylum first in Oxford and then in Cambridge, in the twelfth and thirteenth centuries. Here Peterhouse, the oldest college, was founded by the Bishop of Ely in 1284 – two or three decades at most later than the believed date of Oxford's University College. From the beginning, there was the closest possible association between the monastic foundations and those primarily for scholars. The two universities exemplify this to perfection.

To wander leisurely through the streets of Cambridge, in and out of the velvet-turfed quadrangles, is to be surrounded by all that is finest in medieval and subsequent architecture. An aerial viewpoint shows at a glance how close-set these superb buildings are: Christ's College, known in 1439 as 'God's House'; Clare College, known a century earlier as 'University Hall'; Corpus Christi, a mid-fourteenth-century endowment of merchant-burgesses, where Shakespeare's contemporary Kit Marlow was once a student; King's College, founded by Henry VI in 1441, when he also founded Eton. Its huge chapel is regarded by many architect-connoisseurs as among the finest examples of Gothic not only in Cambridge but in all Europe. If one were to seek out the single most perfect view to be obtained anywhere in Cambridge, it would probably be that of King's College Chapel whose turrets and pinnacles soar nearly a hundred feet into the air, high above the finely chimneyed rectangle of neighbouring Clare College, across the wide, smooth-flowing waters of the River Cam.

The river is among Cambridge's most perfect jewels. It is spanned by a succession of beautiful, elegant and classic bridges: Clare College Bridge, for instance, Trinity Bridge, and St John's College 'Bridge of Sighs'. With the gardens flowing down to the river edge we have the famous 'Backs', among the most memorable features of this ancient and lovely university

CANTERBURY

The site on which the city stands has been successively occupied for more than two thousand years. The earliest relics, of the Celts in about 300 BC, are fragments of a palisade recently unearthed beneath Castle Street. The Romans came and went, leaving little more behind them than the foundations on which the still existing medieval walls were later built. The most memorable 'invasion' was by St Augustine, who brought Christianity from Rome in AD 597 and found here 'not Angles but Angels'. He built the first cathedral, which established Canterbury as the 'Metropolitan City of the English Church'. It was largely destroyed in the successive Danish raids, but on its hallowed site was erected, in the early part of the twelfth century (the crypt dates back to AD 1100), the present cathedral, the first (and most will agree the noblest) cathedral to be built in England, the focal point of the Archi-episcopal See of the Primate of All England.

In 1170, Archbishop Thomas à Becket was murdered within its hallowed walls at the instigation of Henry II; as a result, it was for more than three centuries England's premier place of pilgrimage. (The very word 'canter' derives from the brisk, purposeful trot of Chaucer's more affluent pilgrims to the martyr's shrine.) Only one monarch lies buried here: Henry IV, alongside Queen Joan of Navarre. The tomb of the Black Prince, Edward III's son, hero of Crécy and Poitiers, is also here. But the glories, architectural and monumental, of Canterbury's cathedral demand whole books rather than paragraphs even for their bare enumeration.

The city has other riches in full measure. The medieval city walls, for instance, and the magnificent fourteenth-century West Gate, now appropriately housing a museum, regarded as the finest surviving example of a city gate in all England; and the half-timbered, multi-gabled building, The Weavers, whose upper floor overhangs and is reflected in the calm waters of the little River Stour. In Elizabethan times, Huguenot refugees from persecution at home established themselves in many parts of Kent, notably in its capital, where in time they even outnumbered the native inhabitants, and plied their skilled trade. To this day they have their own chapel in the nine-centuries-old crypt. Two thousand years of history lie about you in Canterbury.

CHESTER

A unique city, and for two reasons. First, it is the only city in England whose ancient walls are complete – you may walk round them in a circuit of some two miles – a city whose Roman layout is immediately evident. Its centre is The Cross. From it, in true Roman fashion, four streets run at right angles to one another: Eastgate and Watergate are the original Via Principalis; Bridge Street the original Via Praetoria; Northgate the original Via Decumana. In the cellars of some of the shops, notably in Northgate, may still be seen, *in situ*, the plinths of pillars that formed the colonnade built nearly 2,000 years ago. In a restaurant basement is a Roman hypocaust.

You must, of course, go in search of these. But other Roman relics are immediately apparent as you walk round the russet sandstone walls laid out by them to enclose their city and stronghold on the River Dee, once an important harbour. Near Newgate, close by the wall, is the largest amphitheatre in England; Roman foundations and another hypocaust are near by; just beyond is the great Eastgate, through which the major road from London passed, and passes still. But on the Roman foundations, over the centuries, higher parapets and individual towers were built – more than a score of them. There is King Charles's Tower, from which he allegedly watched the defeat of his forces in 1645; the Goblin Tower and Bonewaldesthorne's Tower, and the Water Tower, which now contains a fine exhibition of medieval Chester as it became. The ancient wall runs close alongside the precincts of St Werburgh's Cathedral.

Chester, also, is unique because of The Rows. These, following the layout of the Roman streets, notably in Eastgate and Bridge Street, are medieval shops set at pavement level but carrying a pavement overhead along which you walk looking into shops set back some ten feet and itself covered because of the overhang of the half-timbered buildings overhead. Short flights of steps at intervals lead you from street level on to these Rows. There is nothing comparable with these anywhere else in England (though now a modern 'shopping precinct' has been established behind them). Here every building is a timbered treasure: shops, restaurants, inns or Bishops' Palace alike. It may be heresy to say so, but even the cathedral, beautiful as it is as you approach it along the ancient wall, is no more memorable than the medieval Rows.

DURHAM CATHEDRAL

Ideally, the city should be viewed from the air. The view would show how the River Wear describes a hairpin-bend, curving tightly round the base of an enormous bluff, a sandstone peninsula, crowned by the twin glories of the cathedral and castle on opposite sides of Palace Green. Not only is the cathedral among the noblest Norman edifices in Europe, it is the most superbly sited of any, at least in England. No other city is so completely dominated, physically as well as spiritually, by its mother church. And Durham is rare, too, if not unique, in that the great Norman castle near it was for centuries the Bishops' Palace – hence the name of the Green. Strangely, the best distant view of castle and cathedral is from the windows of a train approaching the city from the south.

The castle was built in 1072, only six years after the Battle of Hastings, William the Conqueror having soon recognised the value of such a site, commanding a narrow neck of water at the foot of a mighty natural feature. Its Great Hall, built in 1284, is used today by University of Durham students; one table, still in use, is 400 years old, part of the equipment of the fifteenth-century kitchens.

Even more memorable than the Norman castle, however, is the Cathedral Church of Christ and Blessed Mary the Virgin, started in AD 1093 and, astonishingly in view of its mass and its rich detail, completed only forty years later. It stands on the site to which, in AD 995, Benedictine monks from Lindisfarne, fleeing from the Viking raiders, brought the hallowed body of St Cuthbert and laid it to rest in a primitive chapel. It presents a formidable impression of sheer mass, superbly proportioned. The cylindrical nave pillars, for instance, are no less than 22 feet in circumference; they alternate with equally massive compound columns most beautifully carved; exteriorly, notably when viewed from across the river, the great square buttressed towers give a suggestion of sheer strength that is awe-inspiring. This impression of power is given even in detail: on the outside of the north door there is a massive bronze knocker clenching a ring which, when grasped, guaranteed sanctuary to any supplicant. The Sanctuary Book shows that in the space of fifty years 331 criminals, most of them murderers, clasped this ring and were saved from death. Countless other such relics abound.

LINCOLN CATHEDRAL

With the possible exception of Durham, no English cathedral more magnificently dominates a city than this glorious Cathedral Church of St Mary, the third largest in the country after St Paul's and York Minster. Together with the remains of the Norman castle, built in 1068, it is sited on a high plateau rising above the city itself, the *Lindum Colonia* of the Romans' IXth Legion and an important strategic strongpoint for centuries.

As soon as the castle was begun, the Normans began to build the cathedral; seventy years later it was largely destroyed by fire; in 1185 it was almost wholly destroyed – by that rarity in England, an earthquake. Seven years later a Carthusian monk, Bishop Hugh of Avalon, set about rebuilding it. What you see today is his conception, which inspired builders and craftsmen in stone and wood to their finest efforts over the next century and more. St Hugh's shrine is to be found in the Angel Choir; and it is here, too, that you may see the famous little carved 'Lincoln Imp'.

The central tower of this glorious triple-towered Early-English style cathedral rises to over 270 feet; the body of the cathedral below it is nearly 500 feet in length, and may be said to illustrate every aspect of the finest architectural genius that went into its construction. In the vast nave there are no fewer than fourteen giant columns, no two of them identical with one another yet all conforming to the period in which they were designed and matching one another in spirit and conception. At one end of the great North Transept is the magnificent rose window filled with early-thirteenth-century stained glass and known as the Dean's Eye; it is matched by the great window in the South Transept, known as the Bishop's Eye. Through these windows, light strikes downwards on the magnificent Choir Screen and the stone floor.

The cathedral is supremely rich in stonework, glass and carving. It is rich, too, in memorials. In the North Choir aisle there is a memorial to the Elizabethan composer, William Byrd, once organist here; near by is the treasury of diocesan church plate and, more remarkable still, one of only four surviving originals of Magna Carta. But the first (and final) look at Lincoln Cathedral should be taken from a distance, to see it brooding in Gothic glory over the history-filled city it serves.

Norfolk

NORWICH

Sir Nikolaus Pevsner has declared his opinion that 'Norwich has everything'. A wild claim? You must visit the capital of East Anglia to find out for yourself. In its Cathedral Church of the Holy and Undivided Trinity, dating from the end of the eleventh century, though it was not consecrated until 1278, it possesses one of the finest examples of Norman ecclesiastical architecture in the country. Its 315-foot spire is second only to that of Salisbury Cathedral; its cloisters are the largest in England; in the apse there is a Bishop's Throne possibly 1,000 years old; within the cathedral precincts is Norwich School, at which Lord Nelson was a pupil; here, too, is the grave of Nurse Edith Cavell, executed for her principles in the First World War.

But if the cathedral is the city's chief jewel, it is by no means the only one. Dominating the roof-tops a quarter of a mile to the south is the Castle, the enormous stone keep of which dates back to about AD 1160 and is regarded by experts as the noblest structure of its kind after the Tower of London itself. Until the end of last century it served as the prison, but it now houses a museum and a magnificent collection of paintings by members of the so-called Norwich School such as Cotman and Crome. At the foot of the hill dominated by the castle is the old Bridewell, a fourteenth-century merchant's house once used as a short-term gaol for rogues and vagabonds, though it now serves as a museum of rural life and industry.

The city reveals countless signs of its 1,000-year-old history. Elm Hill, for instance, has been skilfully restored to its pristine medieval appearance, cobbles and all. The medieval walls, still to be seen, enclose an area as large as the City of London. The Guildhall, in which 529 Mayors and Lord Mayors presided until 1938, dates back to AD 1407; the Magistrates' Court and the Court of Records still meet here. A much more modern but hardly less interesting feature is the Maddermarket Theatre, rebuilt in the Elizabethan style and used by the famous Norwich Players for more than half a century past. It would take more space than that available to substantiate Sir Nikolaus' claim for the city, but there is not a citizen of proud Norwich who would challenge it, and many who know England really well will agree with him.

OXFORD

The older, by a few decades, of England's two major universities, Oxford probably owes its origin to the arrival in the late twelfth or early thirteenth century of foreign scholars expelled from the Paris Sorbonne. If tradition is to be accepted, it is older still: its oldest college, University College, having allegedly been founded in the ninth century by King Alfred! Whether or no, it is accepted as the doyen among the colleges, certainly dating back at least to the mid-thirteenth century. Others are hardly less ancient. Inappropriately-named New College was founded by William de Wykeham in 1379 (he also founded Winchester School, whose pupils tend to become 'New Coll. Men'); more than a century earlier, Walter de Merton, Bishop of Rochester, founded the college that bears his name, the third oldest Oxford foundation. Christ Church (alias 'The House') was founded by Cardinal Wolsey in 1525 and originally named after him; it overlooks the Thames, here called the Isis, beyond its beautiful meadows; in Tom Quad, named after the bell, Great Tom, in the Gateway Tower, itself named after the Martyr St Thomas, we have by far the most spacious of all the quadrangles.

Many of the colleges are as close set as those in what Oxford men (of whom the author is one) refer to as 'the other university'. Queen's and 'Univ.' face one another across 'The High'; Trinity and her age-old rival, Balliol, overlook 'The Broad'; Exeter, Jesus and Lincoln line such narrow streets as 'The Turl', or occupy some cobbled back street of medieval charm, as Merton does. More spaciously sited, some possess magnificent gardens: St John's, for instance, and Worcester; Wadham again, with its linked quadrangles, the first a 'perfect square' overlooked by the gatehouse in which Sir Christopher Wren, a former undergraduate who was to rebuild St Paul's and others of London's churches, had his room. It leads into an exquisite walled garden whose velvet lawn is shadowed by one of the noblest copper beeches in all England. At the foot of High Street is Christ Church's only valid rival, Magdalen, dating from 1458. Its 144-foot tower, from which the College Chapel choristers welcome the dawn on May Day with a Latin hymn, overlooks the bridge and the alluring waters of the River Cherwell that flow past the gardens and, notably, Addison's Walk among them.

PLYMOUTH

The city's claim to have the finest natural harbour in Europe is hard to challenge; certainly, viewed from the great promontory of the Hoe, on which, traditionally, Drake insisted on completing his game of bowls before defeating the Spanish Armada in 1588, it is immensely impressive both in its extent and in its natural design. It is associated in everyone's mind with some of the greatest names in maritime history. From Plymouth Sound adventurous sea-captains in the golden age of Elizabeth I sailed forth to enlarge the horizons of the then known world. In 1577 Drake, aboard the *Pelican* (later re-named the *Golden Hind*), set out to circumnavigate the globe; four years later he was elected Mayor of Plymouth. In 1587 he left Plymouth to 'singe the King of Spain's beard'; a year later he defeated the Spanish king's great fleet in the English Channel. Thanks to him, to Raleigh, Gilbert, Hawkins and their peers, Plymouth became the British Navy's base, and neighbouring Devonport one of her chief dockyards.

From Plymouth, too, in 1620 sailed the Pilgrim Fathers, to establish themselves in the New World. This historic event is commemorated in the bronze and stone memorial erected on the Mayflower Steps of the Barbican, the old part of the city familiar to Drake. A plaque on a wall of Island House, near by, records the names of passengers and crew of that small ship that made the transatlantic crossing three-and-a-half centuries ago. Another plaque near by commemorates the touch-down, in 1919 – just three centuries later – of the United States Navy seaplane N.C.4 after its transatlantic crossing from west to east.

From the Barbican, with its steep and narrow cobbled streets overlooking the harbour and its stone and timber buildings regarded even in Elizabethan times as 'a mene thing as an inhabitation for fishers', you climb to the Citadel, built by Charles II who, resenting the people's opposition during the Civil War, had its guns trained on the town rather than out to sea. Thence to the famous Hoe itself. Here the dominating feature is Smeaton's Tower. For more than a hundred years, from 1759 to 1882, it was the lighthouse on Eddystone Rock, fourteen miles distant; when the foundations became unsafe, it was removed, for re-erection where it now stands. It epitomises the watchfulness of the old sea-captains for whom this was their base.

SALISBURY CATHEDRAL

This most beautiful cathedral is, in one important respect, unique: alone of all our cathedrals it was built on a site other than the original one selected for it. The first cathedral was built at the fortified site of Old Sarum, two miles to the north of New Sarum, today's Salisbury, by William the Conqueror's nephew. Almost completely wrecked by a phenomenal thunderstorm, the site was abandoned, largely because of its exposure to wind and weather. Tradition has it that a new site was selected by the fall of an arrow shot southwards to the confluence of the Avon with three smaller rivers. There, in 1220, the foundations were laid. Work was continuous and dedicated, and the impression gained of complete unity of design is the result of this unusually swift progress from foundation to consecration, which took place in 1258.

Aerial views reveal another most unusual feature: the cruciform design incorporates two pairs of transepts instead of the customary single pair. Moreover, this cathedral is one of the very few whose overall length (449 feet) can be seen, unbroken, from west end to east. It is a magnificent example of Early English ecclesiastical building, wholly integrated – save for one splendid exception. This is its most notable feature: the 404-foot spire, the highest in the country, which soars with unparalleled grace into the sky, epitome of man's everlasting quest for higher things. It is so ethereally graceful that it is hard to believe that it weighs little short of 5,000 tons. When, in the mid-fourteenth century, it was added to the original structure, it was necessary to strengthen transepts and crossing, which had to bear its thrust, with strainer arches which may be seen incorporated in them to this day. Shortly after this glorious spire was added, the lovely octagonal chapter house and the colonnaded cloisters, the largest of any cathedral in England, were added.

The cathedral contains the usual quota of fan-vaulted ceilings, tombs and memorials. But it contains also another unique feature: a wrought-iron clock mechanism dating back to 1386, which makes it the oldest piece of machinery in England, possibly in the world. It has no dial, but sounds the hours. Carefully cherished after years of neglect in a belfry, it is still, after six centuries, in full working order.

WELLS CATHEDRAL

There are abundant springs hereabouts, and the little market town most probably takes its name from these; water, indeed, part-surrounds its cathedral. Though it ranks among our smaller examples, it compensates for its lack of amplitude by the beauty of its detail. It occupies a site that almost certainly once held a Saxon church; seven chests of bones bearing the names of Saxon bishops on lead plates were found here, and duly re-interred in the choir aisles. Its first stones were laid in about 1180, to form the altar and choir end; the cathedral's most memorable feature, the glorious west front, in effect a vast stone screen designed to display nearly four hundred statues, was built half a century later. The central tower and the Lady Chapel were added in 1318, followed by the south tower at the end of the century and the north tower some forty years later still. Thus two and a half centuries elapsed between the founding and the completion of this jewel among cathedrals. The serene cloister garth dates from the fifteenth and early sixteenth centuries. Beyond this is the Bishop's Palace, partly of the thirteenth century. Here are swans in the moat and they have evolved the charming practice of ringing the episcopal bell beneath a small window in the wall by the drawbridge when they want to be fed. The palace, incidentally, claims to be one of the oldest inhabited houses in England.

The extraordinary richness of the west front's carving is matched by the interior detail. The ornate canopied prebendal tapestried choir stalls, for instance; the fourteenth-century east window of the choir; and the beautiful curve of foot-worn stone steps of the chapter house, up which one can visualise the ghosts of long-dead ecclesiasts making their laborious way, clinging to the wrought-iron handrail beneath the fan-vaulted ceiling whose shapely ribs spring from a central column. But the feature which may linger longest in the visitor's memory is the famous late-fourteenth-century 'astronomical clock', the main face of which is in the north transept. It has an outer 24-hour dial and an inner minute dial, the 'hands' consisting of moving stars; the moon's phases also are shown. Above the dial, a knightly tournament takes place at every hour. In the triforium near by, an odd seated mechanical figure known as Jack Blandiver sounds the quarter-hours with two hammers on a small suspended bell.

Yorkshire

YORK

To anyone who has not been there, York is, quite simply, York Minster, the largest Gothic church in northern Europe; but it is a very great deal more than that. As Eboracum, in AD 71, it was for three centuries the Romans' northern headquarters; Constantine the Great was proclaimed Emperor here. In 1973 it is still the headquarters of Northern Command. Its stone and timber enshrine nineteen hundred years of history. Between those dates it has been the Anglo-Saxon capital, Eoforwic, and the Danish capital-in-England, Jorvik; a number of its streets, or 'gates', testify to this. The Normans took it, and Clifford's Tower and Baile Hill are their memorials, just as Multangular Tower is a Roman relic, part of the wall they built in AD 200. They enlarged the city walls (for York is one of our very few remaining walled towns) to embrace over 260 acres of present-day York, nearly three miles of them can be walked in less than one hour.

This is the most famous, too, of our truly medieval cities. In the Middle Ages it was England's 'Northern Capital', the second city in the land, and the medieval element may be traced widely, and perhaps most notably in The Shambles – originally the '*Fleshammels*' or Street-of-the-Butchers. It has been perfectly preserved, as fine a medieval street as any in Europe. Another such is Stonegate, built on the Romans' *Via Praetoria*; along this, eleven centuries later, thousands of tons of stone were hauled for the building of the Minster, between AD 1220 and 1470.

Dedicated to St Peter, this is the city's crowning glory: a building over 500 feet long and 240 feet wide, its central, or 'lantern', tower the highest in England, soaring to almost 240 feet. It possesses the finest concentration of medieval glass in England, notably in the Five Sisters window and the east window, the largest in the world with over 2,000 square feet of stained glass in it. The view towards it along the city walls is immensely impressive; possibly even more impressive is the view from the top of the Minster towers of the pantiled roofs of the older, medieval, parts of the city. But York is memorable, too, for a host of small details. Guy Fawkes, for instance, was born and went to school here; and the near-legendary highwayman Dick Turpin was executed here. There are often flowers on his humble grave!

ANCIENT MONUMENTS
AND HISTORIC BUILDINGS

Kent

DOVER CASTLE

For 2,000 years Dover, commanding the narrowest crossing of the English Channel, a bare twenty-one miles, has been the most important point of entry to England from Europe. The Romans recognised this and erected a lighthouse and lookout-point here on Castle Hill. It still stands, within the ramparts enclosing the 900-year-old castle surrendered to William the Conqueror by Harold of England. 2,000 years prior to that there had been an Iron Age fort on this same commanding site, utilised by the Romans for their own purposes and developed centuries later by the Normans and their successors down the years. Not one of our innumerable medieval castles can surpass this one in the sheer impressiveness of its site.

The oldest Norman part of the castle is Peverell's Tower, built immediately after the Conquest. The keep, with walls 20 feet thick and nearly 100 feet high, was built by Henry II and wholly dominates the inner bailey, or courtyard. From that day onwards a succession of monarchs strengthened, added to and elaborated the existing structure. Henry III built the magnificent Constable's Gate on the western side of the complex of ramparts and smaller towers. It is an enormous arched gateway flanked by drum-towers, constituting the traditional barbican. The Constable was the Governor, and so important did William the Conqueror deem this castle that he appointed his half-brother, Odo of Bayeux, to the post. This was held four hundred years later by the Duke of York, destined to become Henry VIII; four hundred years later, the Duke of Wellington was Constable; a century later still, though he was not required to take up residence within its ancient walls, the Constable was – Winston Churchill.

Within its precincts may be visited St Thomas à Becket's Chapel; the bedrooms used by monarchs on their state visits; the banqueting hall, with its magnificent array of weaponry; underground tunnels dug in the chalk in 1216 when a French invasion was anticipated, and extended for the same reason during the Napoleonic Wars; a 289-foot well that was here before the castle was built; the church of St-Mary-in-Castra, of Anglo-Saxon origin, for which the Roman lighthouse served as bell-tower. From earliest times, through nine centuries, Dover Castle has been garrisoned.

FOUNTAINS ABBEY
(3 miles S-W. of Ripon)

Superlatives are always a risk: anything declared to be the largest, finest, oldest, most famous, or whatever will almost invariably be stoutly challenged. Not so, however, in the case of this superlatively fine Ancient Monument. Of all the scores of priories and abbeys still to be found in England, in varying states of preservation, variously sited, Fountains must be awarded the palm; if you had time to see but one in the whole country, this should be your choice. Connoisseurs unhesitatingly call it 'the greatest abbey in England', and particularise their statement by adding that it is the most glorious example of a Cistercian monastery to have survived in this country. Once visited, its impact and its aftermath can never be wholly lost.

Not only does it give a clearer, more convincing picture of what such monastic establishments looked like in their heyday during the long centuries that ended with Henry VIII's ruthless edict that led to the Dissolution of the Monasteries in 1536; it happens also to be one of the most perfectly sited of all our abbeys, Tintern, in Monmouthshire, being perhaps its closest rival in this respect. The vast spread of its buildings lies on either side of the little River Skell, which flows leisurely down Skelldale; the spring which supplied the dissident Benedictine monks when they first came here, in 1132, was to give its name to this great abbey they eventually built. They channelled the water most skilfully so that it flowed beneath and through a series of stone tunnels that automatically supplied running water for their kitchens and latrines and *lavatoria* in which they performed their ablutions; to this day, as then, it imparts a sense of life to the silent grey stonework of the ancient abbey.

No other ruins show more clearly the layout of these monastic establishments. The walls of the now roofless church are 360 feet long; the north transept is still dominated by a seven-storey, 170-foot high tower, the creation of the fifteenth-century Abbot Huby; chapter house and cloisters, the multi-arched *cellarium*, the brothers' refectory and dormitories, the infirmary, warming-room and kitchens: all these, though largely in ruins, can be seen today in that setting of perfection, presenting a picture that must remain indelibly imprinted on the memory, never to be forgotten.

Northumberland

HOUSESTEADS
(Off B 6318, 15 miles N-W. of Hexham)

In Hadrian's Wall England possesses one of the most spectacular relics in Europe of the Roman Empire. The emperor had it built during the decade AD 122–132 as the northern demarcation-line of the empire, spanning England from the North Sea to Solway Firth, an overall distance of 73 miles, though the western end was never completed. Much of it followed the Great Whin Sill, the dramatic ridge of basalt that is so striking a feature of this most northerly of our counties. It was designed as a wall of quarried stone blocks fifteen feet high, with a northward-facing parapet, and seven feet thick. A deep ditch below its north face emphasised its height. Behind it ran a military access-road, and behind that the *vallum*, a deep, wide ditch for added security from rear attack. At intervals of 1,000 paces – the Roman 'mile' – were mile-castles established as look-out points, permanently manned. At longer intervals were fortified camps with garrisons of varying numbers. Of these, Housesteads, probably known to the Romans as Borcovicium, was the largest. It is also the one that has been most thoroughly excavated and, where necessary, rehabilitated.

It covers five acres and accommodated 1,000 men. Its north face forms a continuation of the actual wall and spans the cleft that carries Knag Burn across the line of the wall, which the Roman engineers channelled into a culvert. It majestically overlooks Crag Lough and Greenlee Lough lying at the foot of the basalt precipice. Here you can see and understand how these garrisons lived and operated. The gateways still show the ruts carved in the stone by chariot and wagon wheels. The barracks and granaries, the officers' baths (complete with stone cisterns and piped outflows), the hospital and other ancillary buildings vital to so large an isolated community: all this may be seen and studied *in situ*. A museum with its exhibits enlightens further. Near the south gate, by which you enter from the road, is evidence of a civil community established near the military one: an inn, a shop or two, and – a somewhat macabre feature – the so-called 'Murder House' in which were found the skeletons of a woman and a man, the latter with a sword-blade between his ribs. Abandoned *circa* AD 383, this site remains enormously impressive in the grandeur of its isolation.

Cornwall

LAND'S END

In spite of the 'First-and-Last-in England' hotels, inns and souvenir-shops, this southwesternmost tip of England retains an aura of magic that no commercialism could wholly destroy. The road ends within a few hundred yards of the summit of this huge, jagged assembly of russet-grey, clean-cut granite slabs, cleft horizontally and vertically, against whose base the eternally restless Atlantic waters surge and retreat and return to the attack. In his 'Tour through the Whole Island of Great Britain' Defoe wrote: 'Nature has fortify'd this part of this island in a strange manner, as if she knew the force and violence of the mighty ocean.' If he were to revisit this country two-and-a-half centuries after writing those words he would find no reason to modify them. Even on a calm day, the scene is impressive; on a day of gales and lashing rain it can be terrifying. There have been more ship-wrecks hereabout than in any other stretch of our long, indented coastline.

Immediately off shore, granite masses project from the turbulent waters, unmoved by their power. Over the past two hundred years they have acquired names; some of these, such as 'Dr Johnson's Head', singularly apt. Another is curiously named 'Dr Syntax'; another, part-hidden beneath an overhang, is the 'Pele' or 'Spire Rock'; hard by is the 'Armed Knight'. A mile off shore there is a jagged reef on which stands the famous Longships lighthouse, erected there with enormous labour and risk in 1797. Eight miles out to sea is the Wolf Rock, with its own isolated lighthouse. Twenty-odd miles farther out to sea, to the south-west, are the Isles of Scilly.

Danger ever-present on the surface; romance, however, on the hidden sea bed. For here, according to a tradition that will not lie down and die, is the legendary Land of Lyonesse that once (they say, and older Cornishmen still believe) occupied the region between the Isles of Scilly and the bastion we know as Land's End. Here, if we accept the tradition, there were once as many as 146 churches, and a population large enough to fill them on Holy Days. But the churches and other buildings and all the inhabitants of fabled Lyonesse were swallowed up by an inundation caused by the conflict between the English Channel to the south and the mightier Atlantic Ocean. No date is given. But from such a grandstand as this it must have been a spectacular sight.

Cheshire

LITTLE MORETON HALL
(On A 34, 3 miles S-W. of Congleton)

Known also as Moreton Old Hall, this is without question one of the finest examples of 'magpie', or black-and-white, half-timbered buildings in England. Its alternative name is more appropriate, for it is so old that subsequent alterations are dated 1559 and signed on a window beam 'Richard Dale, Carpeder' – a craftsman obviously proud of his handiwork. It has been aptly described as 'native Gothic lightly touched by the first flush of the Renaissance'. Standing in open meadow land, it is surrounded on all four sides by a square moat. In itself it is a tall, rectangular, heavily gabled structure set about a cobbled courtyard, one side so designed as to reveal the gardens beyond. You enter by way of a stone bridge spanning the moat, and it is from this south-west approach that the classic view can best be appreciated, the soaring timbers being beautifully reflected in the still water between the grassy banks.

Exterior and quadrangle aspects alike are a mass of variegated high gables, stepped outwards on supporting oak brackets intricately carved and inset with plaster-work which, uniquely here, is subordinated to the timberwork. Leaded panes of varying sizes and shapes add much to the 'secret' feel of the place exteriorly. Within, the upper storeys are reached by way of several staircases that spring from near the impressive gatehouse. Some rooms are spacious; others so small that one wonders what purpose they could have been designed to serve. In one of these, a sliding panel in the multi-panelled walls gives access to a secret room filling the space behind a wide chimney-breast. Some maintain that this is the traditional 'priest's hide'; in fact there is an even more secret chamber than this one, below moat level and attainable only by way of a long, twisting, underground tunnel.

The larger chambers are very impressive: the 68-foot Long Gallery, for instance, with its huge fireplaces bearing the Royal Arms of both France and England; and the great Banqueting Hall, served from a kitchen with a hearth capacious enough to roast an ox whole – as was certainly the practice in Tudor times. The lofty gables and undulating roof-line tend to make Moreton Old Hall look top-heavy; but it has stood here for four-and-a-half centuries and looks good for as long again, especially as it is under the dedicated care of the National Trust.

74

Wiltshire

STONEHENGE
(Off A 344, 3 miles W. of Amesbury)

This megalithic complex is acknowledged to be the most remarkable of its type, not merely in England, a country singularly rich in relics of the Neolithic and earlier ages, but in the world. More research has been devoted to this site than to any other; much has been established as 'almost certainly' true, but much still remains for archaeologists to ascertain by probing this mysterious and intractable secret.

In the seemingly limitless, undulating landscape of Salisbury Plain you are confronted by a complex array of gigantic megaliths enclosed within a bank and a ditch. They form concentric circles and ovals of enormous rough-hewn sarsen, or local sandstone, columnar blocks, some tilted or even prone, others grouped as towering trilithons – twin pillars capped with massive lintels fitted in the fashion of primitive but workmanlike mortice-and-tenon: rounded knobs inserted into cup-like recesses. Closer examination reveals a distinct difference in the types of stone used. In addition to the local sarsens, which proliferate on Salisbury Plain, there are the huge 'blue-stones' which geologists have established could not have emanated from anywhere nearer than the Prescelly Mountains of Pembrokeshire on the far side of the Severn Estuary. The mind boggles at the problems that faced the successive generations of builders of this unique prehistoric monument, not merely in elevating these megaliths into position but in dragging them cross-country over a distance which, even in a straight line, would substantially exceed 150 miles.

Archaeologists have established that, from start to completion, the building of this monumental complex must have occupied at least 900 years, from 2200 BC onwards. This disposes of the belief that the Druids built it, still maintained by the annual Midsummer Eve ceremonies enacted here that culminate in the moment when the sun rises over the Hele (or Sun) Stone, for the Druids did not reach these shores until more than 1,000 years later. They may indeed have 'taken over' Stonehenge, but its original purpose remains speculation. However, so vast an undertaking must have been inspired by pagan-religious fervour as well as something functional. In fact, it can be proved, now, to have been a remarkably sophisticated device for measuring the all-important seasons: a form of 'perpetual calendar' on a majestic, awe-inspiring scale.

76

Monmouthshire

TINTERN ABBEY
(5 miles N. of Chepstow)

The various Orders that built England's abbeys laid down certain pre-requisites relating to the sites on which they were to stand. Some, notably the Cistercians, insisted that their monasteries were to be situated as far as was practicable 'in places removed from human habitation'. Furness Abbey in Lancashire is a good example of this; Whalley Abbey is another in the same county; and Byland Abbey in neighbouring Yorkshire. Some abbeys were built on lofty sites, as though their occupants wished to be that much nearer heaven than they would be in valley sites. Two such examples are the Benedictine Abbey at Tynemouth, which stands on a fortified headland overlooking the bleak North Sea; another such Benedictine foundation is Whitby Abbey, which stands isolated on the massive East Cliff half a mile from the little seaport that gave it its name. There is no more spectacularly sited abbey anywhere in the country.

A perfect contrast is Tintern Abbey, set on level greensward in a crook of the meandering River Wye, a Cistercian foundation exactly contemporary with Fountains Abbey in far-away Yorkshire. True, there is a hamlet of a few hundred souls a mile or so distant, but this secluded site on the right bank of the Wye is screened by steeply-rising, thickly tree-clad ground that isolates it today as much as it has done over the long centuries that have flowed over it. The earliest church built here is no longer to be seen. The stone skeleton confronting you today is mainly of the thirteenth century. The abbey church, roofless but still retaining its superb arches at each end of choir and nave and transepts, is the focal point. There are the remains, too, of the other traditional buildings: cloisters, dormitories, refectories, the all-important abbot's house, and so forth.

A relatively unusual feature here is that, owing to the close proximity of the river, the cloister and other buildings were set out on the north rather than the more usual south side. Though there was running water so close to them that the buildings can be seen beautifully reflected in it, the water used by the monks came from a spring on the south side. It is still, and appropriately, known as Coldwell. This is indeed one of the most beautiful, serenest abbey sites in England; it possesses a haunting quality that can be deeply felt but defies description.

78

SHOW TOWNS AND VILLAGES

Sussex

AMBERLEY
(Off B 2139, 5 miles N. of Arundel)

In the whole of East and West Sussex combined, it would be hard to discover a village more wholly charming than this one. It has the good fortune to lie off a secondary road which has already branched off a main road, so that though traffic speeds by not a mile from it, the village has remained quite unspoiled. A single narrow road runs through it, to peter out almost in the shadow of the remains of a Norman castle and, quite close to this, the Norman Church of St Michael. The oldest parts of both church and castle are indeed Norman – the zigzag moulding of the chancel arch, among the most beautiful in the county, is evidence of this so far as the church is concerned, though most of its fabric dates only from the thirteenth and fourteenth centuries. As for the castle: much of it was destroyed during the Civil War, but the fine fourteenth-century gatehouse still stands for all to see.

But the village itself, though it possesses no particularly outstanding feature apart from the church and castle, is perhaps in its way more memorable than either: for its extraordinary atmosphere of serenity, and for the impression it gives of complete integration. The cottages are of mellow stone, lit by woodwork in various harmonising colours and roofed with well-laid thatch. Some of them stand high above road level, their old-world gardens sloping down to the tops of stone walls eight or ten feet high, so that the flowers appear to the passer-by looking up at them as though they grow out of the upper stonework. Other cottages are at road level and close alongside; these are part-screened from such traffic as goes past them by low, hollow walls filled like elongated troughs with colourful flowers: a sort of plinth, part man-made, part the work of nature.

Trees overhang parts of the road. To the north rise the South Downs, screening the village from the colder winds, so that here the warmth seems permanent In fact, Amberley occupies a longish, narrow terrace; from any cottage window, from the single road, or from the seat with a plaque announcing that it has won prizes for being the 'Best-kept Village in Sussex', you look out to the south and west across water-meadows kept fertile by the serpentining River Arun as it flows southwards to Arundel and the sea a few miles beyond.

BOSCASTLE
(Off B 3263, 5 miles N-W. of Camelford)

Until about 1890 this was quite a busy little port; today, in spite of its sturdy stone quay, it is difficult to think of it as anything but a 'natural' feature of the most dramatic stretch of coastline in England. The tiny hamlet itself seems to have shrunk back from it, to hide inland. Its inhabitants are largely the descendants of the men who at one time made their living from the sale of culled seals caught in the caves at sea level beneath the slate outcrops; this was once the hamlet's economy. Two small, swiftly-flowing streams, the Valency and the Jordan, flow down off the glen and converge at the point where they meet the in-flowing tide; it is at this point that the builders established their curving stone quay. All for the most part appears deserted; here, you are 'out of this world'; you have left the road and approach the harbour on cliffside tracks for the last few hundred yards, a walk which it is well worth taking both leisurely and with circumspection, for the cliffs are Cornish cliffs. An hour before low tide every day you can see, just beyond the harbour, what appears to be a geyser. In fact it is an explosion of sea-water bursting upwards from one of Cornwall's many blow-holes; on a day of rough seas it is an impressive performance, continuously repeated.

You can continue to walk along the cliff paths on either side of this little estuary, winding like a miniature Norwegian fjord, until you come to the open Atlantic. Looming above you all the time is Forrabury Common, with its squat, ancient church, parts of which are Norman. This is National Trust property, and so is secure from exploitation and commercialism for all time. If the oldest parts of this lonely church date back 1,000 years, this common, overlooking the harbour and winding waterway, possesses signs of an even more ancient occupation. Centuries before the coming of the Normans, the Celts established themselves here. On this rough-turfed cliff-top, if you know what to look for and how to find them, there survive to this day relics of what are technically known as 'stitches': actually cultivation-strips first carved out and sown by the Celts and used by later generations down the centuries for growing their sparse crops. Indeed, this unobtrusive little place is rich in revelations of a way of life that flourished here more than a thousand years ago.

BRIGHTON

No one would seriously dispute the town's claim to be England's premier seaside resort. Seven miles of beaches and two internationally famous piers, one of them a century old, superficially account for its popularity. But there is much more here than beaches, century-old Aquarium, the newer Dolphinarium and the countless other forms of entertainment; Brighton is, *par excellence*, the finest example we have of a Regency town. Originally a humble fishing village long since engulfed by the restless sea that has eroded the chalk cliffs of England for aeons, 'Brighthelmstone' was first put on the map by Dr Richard Lewis who, in 1754, prescribed bathing in and drinking sea-water as a panacea for 'feverish infection', for 'strengthening and bracing the muscular fibres', and indeed for almost all known ills. Thirty years later, the Prince of Wales, 'Prinny' (eventually to become George IV), paid Brighthelmstone a visit, liked the place, commissioned a 'marine residence' there, moved in, and thus set the seal of royal approval on the first seaside resort; it has never looked back.

The classically designed residence was soon re-built in 'Indian Moghul' style with spires, minarets and onion-domes, an arresting looking structure known for a century and a half as the Royal Pavilion. George IV occupied it regularly; William IV did likewise; and even Queen Victoria – until she made the curious discovery that it 'lacked privacy'! Today it is a public building, an oriental looking treasure house in which memorable exhibitions are held the year round but perhaps chiefly noteworthy within for the strong Chinese emphasis of the décor which 'Prinny' delighted in: the astonishing Banqueting Hall, for instance, the Music Room with its amazingly elaborate chandeliers, and the King's Bedroom itself.

The true Regency aspect of the town, however, is to be seen in the streets and squares and fine buildings that line and overlook them: Kemp Town and the Brunswick Estate are outstanding examples, but you will find individual expressions of the age almost everywhere. Not, however, amid The Lanes, where the seventeenth-century fishermen's cottages of Brighthelmstone were situated. Today they offer a happy hunting-ground for the seeker after antiques and curios in a very picturesque setting.

Worcestershire

BROADWAY
(On A 44, 5 miles S-E. of Evesham)

This, 'the perfect village', lies just over the border of Gloucestershire which, with Oxfordshire, contains practically the whole of the delectable 500-mile-square region we know as The Cotswolds. Connoisseurs may prefer hamlets such as Coln St Aldwyns and Ampney St Mary; Ruskin, no mean judge, regarded Bibury as 'without peer'. But to see a Cotswold township of some 2,000 inhabitants that cannot be faulted and is absolutely typical, Broadway certainly justifies its claim.

It is a place of consistently beautiful, largely four-centuries-old buildings of the local oolitic limestone. They line the wide Main Street (the 'broad way') on either side, separated from it by smooth, well-tended turf which perfectly sets off the mellow honey-hued façades beneath their fine slab roofs and delicately proportioned gables and dormer windows. The street climbs gently towards Fish Hill and so to the eighteenth-century 'Folly' known as Beacon Tower, from the top of which, at 1,000 feet, you may see westwards beyond Worcester Cathedral and Tewkesbury Abbey and northwards beyond Stratford-upon-Avon to Warwick Castle: a magnificent panorama.

Every individual building is a precious stone, perfectly set. The *Lygon Arms* (formerly the *White Hart*) is one of the most famous as well as beautiful hostelries in England; in contrast, there is the *Broadway*, timber-built and therefore standing out amid the limestone that characterises almost every building in the Cotswolds. Perfectly integrated as a village, and perhaps most remarkable for this very factor, nevertheless every individual building, large and small, merits the closest inspection. Here symmetry and proportion have reached their apotheosis, whether in balance of frontage with gable-end, of mullion with transom, of dormer with chimney-stack or doorway with window. The place exudes an aura of established peace as well as charm; if ever a place may be said to have acquired character, even personality, over the centuries, it is Broadway. The only criticism that could possibly be levelled against it (and even if just, it is unkind) is that it is perhaps a little self-conscious, too much aware of itself. But then, does not perfection entitle a place, as it does a beautiful woman, to be more than a little conscious of its special attributes?

86

Wiltshire

CASTLE COMBE
(Off B 4039, 5 miles W. of Chippenham)

This has been well termed the 'village in a nutshell'. The immediate impression it gives is of extreme compactness. Three small roads slant down into it from wooded slopes, to converge in a small triangular square whose hub is a thirteenth-century stepped market cross beneath a roof of steeply pitched slates topped by a neat finial, the whole supported on four graceful stone pillars. Facing one another across this focal point are the two old inns, *The Castle* and *The White Hart*, at which one may guess that vendors drank and made merry after each day's buying and selling. In the background, a little above the village centre, is the thirteenth-and-later-century Church of St Andrew with a fine mid-fifteenth-century tower erected 'at the expense of the clothiers of the district' – for the village lies on the fringe of the true Cotswold sheep-farming and wool-processing country. A reminder of this is to be found at the foot of the street that runs down to the little By Brook. Here you will find the medieval Weavers' House. Returning to the church, up the hill, you will find if you look keenly enough further reminders of the importance of the place: there are in the stonework of the tower carvings of shuttles and other weavers' implements dating from the latter part of the sixteenth century when the trade was in full swing.

From the bridge over the stream you will obtain the best view of the village as a whole, by common consent of those who know England intimately among the half-dozen most beautiful in the country. The cottages are all of the limestone that is the glory of the Cotswolds. Here it is not of quite so golden a hue as in Gloucestershire and Oxfordshire, it is slightly greyer in tone, but the texture is as beautiful as ever, changing as the sun strikes full or aslant upon the stonework. The steeply pitched slab roofs carry russet lichen that imparts warmth to them; the dormers and small gables, the mullions and transoms and dripstones: all these are here in profusion, framing the small, secretive windows, all different yet all blending in style one with the other to form an integrated whole. Virginia creeper proliferates on some gable-ends; the fine church tower rises above the roofs and chimneys, and is itself silhouetted against the banks of trees that clothe the slopes at whose feet this exquisitely proportioned village lies in a three-dimensional, natural frame.

Devonshire

CLOVELLY
(Off A 39, 10 miles W. of Bideford)

There are many 'show' villages in most areas of England, each with its individual claim to distinction; there is only one village that is truly unique, and this is to be found in the north-west corner of this county which itself possesses perhaps an unfair number of extremely picturesque villages. Its single street is not in fact a street at all; it is a series of slanting cobbled steps that, in a quarter of a mile, drop from the car park above it some 400 feet down to the curved stone quay that half-enwraps the shingled beach washed by the usually gentle waters of Barnstaple Bay. No wheeled traffic is possible. If you are energetic (and sure-footed) you walk from top to bottom – always remembering that you have then to walk back uphill to your starting-point! Or you may hire a donkey, whose tiny hooves will go clitter-clatter up and down the cobbles, as its ancestors' have done for the four hundred years that Clovelly has been a fishing-port. Apart from the sea, this is the only means of access to the village, for human beings and for their provisions and their exports alike.

On either side of these cobbled steps are cottages, each set a 'step' lower than its neighbour; their façades are white-painted, their woodwork gleaming black, like the capstones that many of their enclosing walls carry. Most windows are filled with troughs of bright flowers. From the upper ones, that project across the cobbles, the occupants can practically shake hands over your head, so close do they approach one another. At the foot of the hill is the 300-year-old *Red Lion*, from a nineteenth-century owner of which Charles Kingsley took his character Salvation Yeo for his book, *Westward Ho!* It is from here, or from the quay, that the best view may be obtained.

Clovelly lies in the heart of a cleft, the steep sides of which climb to the skies, thickly clad with trees, so that it seems to be enfolded by the tender hand of Nature herself. Though it faces north, and out over open water, the village has the 'feel' rather of a South Devon village, basking in warmth, surrounded by lush vegetation, as though it was situated at the head of one of those sheltered estuaries that are so characteristic of the opposite coastline of this, England's second largest county. Yet, as any local man will tell you, Barnstaple Bay waters can be threatening.

DUNSTER
(Off A 39, 3 miles E. of Minehead)

The High Street of this unspoiled village is wider than those of many towns – comparable with Marlborough's High Street or Oxford's St Giles. It is lined on both sides with buildings large and small, of brick, stone, timber, tile and thatch, many of them very old indeed, few of them more recent than the early eighteenth century, all of them individually memorable and beautifully integrated one with another. At the upper end of the street, on an 'island site', stands the uniquely proportioned yarn market, built about 1589 when this was an important cloth centre. The steeply-pitched octagonal roof, with its gabled dormer windows, is supported on squat, sturdy pillars set in a massive plinth. Almost immediately opposite is *The Luttrell Arms*, now a hotel of character, though the discerning eye readily detects that it was built for a different purpose. It was, in fact, the residence of the Abbot of Cleeve, and its fine porch and other less immediately apparent features indicate its medieval origin.

Towering above and beyond the lower end of the street are the castellated walls and towers of Luttrell Castle, rising from amid their plinth of close-set trees. It was founded just after the Norman Conquest and has been occupied since 1070. The Luttrell family, who now own it, and whose name is borne by the former abbot's residence, have occupied it since the year 1375, and live there still, though there was a brief period during the Civil War when, as Parliamentarians, they were temporarily ousted by the Royalists – only to return and settle down for a further three centuries. The feudal 'feel' of Dunster is largely due to the dominance of this castle.

Branching westwards from the foot of the wide street you should explore the narrow lanes. Overlooking one of these is a medieval house with overhanging upper storeys which was once a nunnery. Near by is the old Castle Mill, with a rare type of water-wheel; a pack-horse bridge spans the stream that once turned the wheel. Continue along one of these half-hidden lanes and you will find yourself at the lower end of a track that winds its way upwards into terrain that lies between Exmoor proper and the Brendon Hills. Pack-horse trains made their way along this route when Dunster was a busier little place than it is today.

FINCHINGFIELD
(On B 1053, 9 miles N. of Braintree)

This is one of the handful of villages whose claim to be 'the most picturesque in all England' is really difficult to challenge; more than one of its close rivals will be found in these pages, making the same baffling claim. In this instance, the picturesqueness derives in almost equal degree from the appearance of the buildings of which it is composed and Nature's contribution in the character of its site.

The houses 'step' downwards on a gentle slope from the crown of a low hill that is itself surmounted by the Church of St John the Baptist, its Norman tower capped with an elegant eighteenth-century cupola. Close by the church is a cluster of almshouses, formerly the Guildhall, dating back to about AD 1500. On the other side is Hill House, whose five barge-boarded gables give it at once an impressive and a gracious appearance. Another fine house, a contrast to the modest cottages whose russet-tiled and thatched roofs lend warmth and cosiness to the scene, is Spains Hall, an Elizabethan building on the outskirts of the village once occupied by William Kempe who observed a seven-years' silence as a self-imposed penance for falsely accusing his wife. He died in 1628, and you may see his monument in the church after passing through the Norman West Doorway surmounted by two sculpted human heads flanking a goat's head. Indeed, the church is a repository of memorable features.

The village street curves downwards to a little green and, below that, the white-railed pond, across which the best photographs of this charming little place are usually taken. It is in fact a still backwater of the little River Pant, cruising territory of a swan or two and a covey of ducks, the rail just the right height for one to lean over it and contemplate leisurely the serenity of the scene spread outwards and upwards beyond the water, the white facades of the cottages and smaller houses, capped by the squat tower, its cupola and weathervane. To the left of the pond is the *Green Man* inn, its signboard swung from a beautiful wrought-iron bracket; not far away, though not visible from this stance, is one of the few remaining post-mills, of white-painted weather-boarding in the regional tradition. The term 'hunched-up' has been used to describe this village, but it is not really appropriate here.

GRASMERE
(Off A 591, 6 miles N-W. of Windermere)

The few houses of this small village cluster at the north end of the lake that shares its name. Most famous among these, of course, is Dove Cottage, the home from 1799 to 1808 of William Wordsworth and his sister Dorothy. Though none of the buildings have any great architectural merit, Words-worth himself – who knew the English Lakes as few men before or since his day have known them – pronounced it 'the loveliest spot that man hath ever found', and the poet Gray called it 'a little unsuspected paradise'. To dis-cover whether their praise is deserved, you must see it for yourself, and leisurely, too, for it is the 'feel' of Grasmere as well as its setting that makes it so memorable. The lake is on its doorstep, virtually an integral part of the village; Helm Crag, Butter Crag and Nab Scar dominate it from not so very far away.

Dove Cottage dates from the seventeenth century and was once an inn. Its interest today lies in the fact that it was the home of a major poet and his sister and a meeting-place of literary figures such as de Quincey and Robert Southey, and Coleridge, who followed his fellow-poet to the Lakes and 'drank tea on the island in lovely Grasmere Lake, our kettle hanging from the branch of a fir-tree'. To pass through the doorway of Dove Cottage today is to enter into the company of poets' ghosts.

Every August Grasmere becomes temporarily the venue for a very different type of company: the village is then the setting for the famous Lakeland Sports, of competitive running and jumping, of the generations-old tradition of Cumberland-Westmorland style wrestling and, most spectacular of all, the annual Guides' Race up the steep slope of 1,500-foot Butter Crag, along its ridge, and down its formidable scree back to the arena; there is no comparable spectacle in all England, and it is small wonder that 20,000 people come to it from all parts of the country and farther afield too. The great occasion over, the little village settles down to its age-old calm; the visitors continue to come, but in smaller numbers. They are con-cerned with gentler pursuits: to visit reverently the home of a man who wrote some supremely great nature poetry and inspired those who followed him. He is buried, with his sister, his wife and his daughter, in the churchyard of St Oswald's, where an annual Rush-bearing ceremony is still held.

LAVENHAM
(On B 1070, 6 miles N. of Sudbury)

This most beautiful minor township owes its existence to the cloth trade that flourished in this county from the mid-fourteenth to the mid-sixteenth century. Its many irregularly laid-out streets – Barn Street, Lady Street, Prentice Street, Water Street and Shilling Street in particular – like the once-important Market Place, are lined with half-timbered buildings, notably the famous Wool Hall, every one of which is a reminder of the wealth as well as the craftsmanship that went to its construction three, four hundred years ago. Among the most memorable of these is the Guildhall (scheduled, like the Market Cross, as an Ancient Monument), which was erected at the time of the formation of the Guild of Corpus Christi, as long ago as 1529. One of its massive corner-posts carries a representation by some skilled wood-carver of the day of the 15th Lord de Vere; he is recalled again in the lovely de Vere House in Church Street – one of a group of houses most of which are known only by their street numbers today, though each is remarkable for some distinctive individual feature. Some of Lavenham's houses, like those of neighbouring Clare, are noteworthy for the beautiful pargetting of their plasterwork, a feature seen at its best in Suffolk.

On the outskirts of the village, dominating it from a bluff that overlooks it, is the famous 'Wool' church, dedicated to SS Peter and Paul, built (as the term implies) with money derived from the region's basic industry of the day, endowed by men such as de Vere who chose this most appropriate method of returning thanks to their Maker for their prosperity. There is medieval carving within; there is sixteenth-century sculpture, quite possibly by Flemish craftsmen; the fan-vaulting of its notable south porch was the gift of an earlier de Vere, 13th Earl of Oxford. But the outstanding feature of this great church is its enormous square buttressed tower of flint and stone quoins that soars more than 140 feet into the air, dwarfing the nave, a landmark for miles in all directions. Its tenor bell, cast in 1625, is considered to be one of the finest-toned in Europe, and celebrates its own birthday annually on 21 June. There are other 'Wool' churches in Suffolk (as also in the Cotswolds): at neighbouring Kersey, for instance; few of them rival Lavenham's in stature.

LOWER SLAUGHTER
(Off A 429, 3 miles S. of Stow-on-the-Wold)

Impossible to locate any place that more completely belies the apparent significance of its name! Unthinkable that ever strife, let alone violent death, could have taken place amid the serenity of this Cotswold hamlet, set in the Windrush Valley. A line of cottages, each behind its slope of velvety turf leading to the bright waters of a tributary stream spanned by a succession of lightweight, white-painted foot-bridges: here is serenity epitomised, personified; time virtually stands still; no road of any importance passes through it; at the far end, the stream curves leisurely round the village green, planted with ash, limes and beech trees that embower the old well house; opposite, screened from view, is the modest manor house, built of course of the oolitic limestone characteristic of the Cotswolds throughout. In the little church (elaborately restored) may be seen an arcade that dates from the twelfth century.

The origin of the name, which it shares with its neighbour, Upper Slaughter, a mile or two away, is probably a corruption of 'slough' – low-lying, marshy ground; certainly there is much water threading lush water-meadows hereabouts. At the near end of the hamlet, at the junction of the main stream and a diminutive offshoot, the old mill stands. Its original function has long been superseded by the ubiquitous van-delivered wrapped loaf; but steps have been taken to preserve it and from time to time the mill-wheel slowly turns as the sluices are temporarily raised, adding a touch of life to a scene which, by contrast with most centres of population however small, seems to hover perpetually on the fringe of wakefulness – or sleep.

True, Lower Slaughter has been 'discovered' and there are days in high summer when visitors flock to it to test the truth of what they have been told. But its magic is such that clamour is instinctively subdued; the peace is hardly disturbed. You will have to look hard, even in the five hundred or so square miles that constitute this incomparable region, to find another village where the interplay of water and sloping turf, trees and the cottages they shadow, can be matched. One parallel that may spring to the mind of anyone who has explored the lesser-known villages of the Netherlands is the enchanting and ever-memorable 'water village' of Giethoorn.

SHERE
(Off A 25, 6 miles W. of Dorking)

Midway between Dorking and the county town of Surrey, Guildford, and little more than twenty miles from London, there is a cluster of quite enchanting villages each of which has retained its individuality in spite of pressures and threats of development all about them. Peaslake, Abinger Hammer, Gomshall, Friday Street, Albury and Farley Green: each of these is a small oasis of delight, close to the metropolis yet within easy reach of Leith Hill and its great beech forest. There is also Shere, the most perfect of them all; a village of character as well as of charm. Happily, it has been as successfully bypassed as Chilham in Kent, and sleeps on, undisturbed.

Lying in a hollow, it is approached from three directions by sloping, narrow lanes whose earth banks, often rising to a dozen feet and more and probably carved out by pack-horse trains travelling leisurely hither and yon over the years, are topped by stands of beech trees, outliers of the massed legions of their fellows that clothe so much of the higher ground hereabouts, culminating in Leith Hall itself. Through the heart of the village trickles the Tillingbourn, beneath a small bridge or two, overlooked by trees and some of the sixteenth- and seventeenth-century cottages and shops, some of them tile-hung, other half-timbered, the timbers in-filled with brick or plaster or both, their small, secret windows lead-paned in rectangular or diamond patterns. They line the single street that climbs gently, to open out into a diminutive square overlooked by the Church of St James.

Early Transitional, it is eight centuries old and stands amid its spacious tree-embowered graveyard on the site of a much earlier, Saxon, church. Its fabric is the mingled stone and flint of many such buildings in the south-east; it is capped by a beautifully proportioned broach spire, more common in neighbouring Sussex than Surrey. Whereas many churches, notably in Suffolk and Somerset, seem disproportionately large for the communities they were built to serve, this church perfectly matches the size of the village it dominates from above. Indeed, it could be said that, quite apart from the picturesque quality of its individual buildings, the outstanding impression one has of Shere is its close-knit, harmonious character; it lies serene, complete in itself, undisturbed by the world that is to be found just beyond its confines.

Warwickshire

STRATFORD-UPON-AVON

This medieval market town in the very heart of England, birthplace of the world's greatest dramatist, comes first, after London, in the list of 'MUSTS' drawn up by almost every visitor to this country. Considering the sweeping changes that have afflicted almost every town in the past few decades, Stratford has remained singularly untouched. Were the sixteenth-century traveller, John Leland, who visited the town twenty years before Shakespeare was born, to re-visit it today he might still write of its 'very lardge stretes', its houses 'reasonably well buyldyd of tymbar', its Church of the Holy Trinity, 'a fayre lardge peace of worke', and the 'right goodly chappell' of the Guild of the Holy Cross adjoining the Grammar School and Almshouses, still to be seen in Church Street. He wrote appreciatively, too, of the magnificent 14-arched bridge, the gift of a citizen who became Lord Mayor of London, Sir Hugh Clopton, after whom it is named; it still carries the majority of visitors across the river into the heart of the town.

But in 1540 he would know nothing of what Stratford means today, for a quarter of a century was to pass before Shakespeare was born, in Henley Street, in a timber-built house now preserved by the Trust that also cares for Anne Hathaway's Cottage at near-by Shottery, where his wife once lived; New Place, purchased by Shakespeare on his retirement and occupied by him until his death in 1616; and other fine examples of half-timbered buildings that he once knew. Stratford *is* Shakespeare. The great actor David Garrick established the Shakespeare Festival there two centuries ago; a Shakespeare Memorial Theatre was opened in 1879, burned down in 1926, and replaced in 1932 by the Royal Shakespeare Theatre, superbly sited on the bank of the broad Avon. Shakespeare's Birthday Celebrations, on St George's Day, 23 April, are attended annually by devotees from all parts of the world.

Stratford has a strong link with the United States. In High Street there is Harvard House, built by Alderman Thomas Rogers in 1596. His daughter Katherine married one Robert Harvard; it was their son who founded Harvard University. Though the house is in Stratford, its deeds belong to that university, the house having been generously presented to it by a citizen of Chicago, Edward Morris, in 1909.

WIDECOMBE-IN-THE-MOOR
(Off A 384, 5 miles N. of Ashburton)

It is hard to believe, unless you approach it from the upper reaches of Dartmoor, that this village, nestling in a hollow, is not very far short of 1,000 feet above sea level. But on all sides of the deep saucer in which it lies, the turf and granite outcrops of the moor rise steadily to something like twice that height. Enclosed by trees, you might hardly suspect, until you actually entered it, that there was a village there at all. But a brave hint is given: the splendid 120-foot pinnacled tower that soars above the fifteenth-century Church of St Pancras alone seems to 'reach for the skies'. Though it is but one church in a county remarkable for its magnificent parish churches, this one is appropriately known as the Cathedral of the Moor.

Widecombe has become famous because of its place in the song about Uncle Tom Cobleigh-and-All (not forgetting the famous Grey Mare). But it is truly remarkable in its own right, deservedly a place of pilgrimage for those in search of the unusual and impressive in granite country. The great church tower, dating from about 1500, was paid for by the local tin miners who had found unexpected prosperity; like the wool merchants of Suffolk and the Cotswolds, they paid tribute to the God who had favoured them. The cottages of the village are grouped about two tree-shaded greens. Close to the church is a building constructed of the characteristic massive granite blocks of the region, known as the Church House, or Sexton's House. Both historically and architecturally it is important enough to have become National Trust property; today it serves in part as the Village Hall and, as such, has returned to a full life.

Granite, of course, predominates here, as it does in all parts of Dartmoor and neighbouring Bodmin Moor. But this small, isolated village is something of an oasis: some unusually fine chestnuts and sycamores grow here lavishly, interspersed among the cottages, their roots occasionally breaking out as though in protest among the granite outcrops of the two small greens. One might think that Nature, for once embarrassed by the prevailing harshness of the rugged skeleton over which the peat and coarse turf of the moor is stretched, had sought to soften it here and there with a touch of living greenery to compensate for the character of the fundamental raw material.

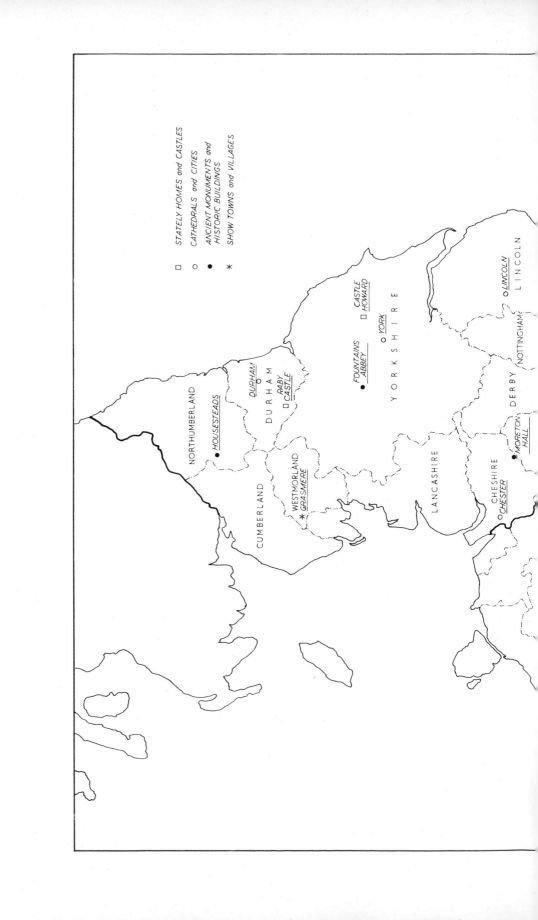

STATELY HOMES and CASTLES

CATHEDRALS and CITIES

ANCIENT MONUMENTS and
HISTORIC BUILDINGS

SHOW TOWNS and VILLAGES

NORTHUMBERLAND

● HOUSESTEADS

CUMBERLAND

WESTMORLAND
GRASMERE
✳

DURHAM
DURHAM
RABY
☐ CASTLE

LANCASHIRE

CHESHIRE
○ CHESTER

● FOUNTAINS
ABBEY

● MORETON
HALL

CASTLE
☐ HOWARD

○ YORK

Y O R K S H I R E

D E R B Y

NOTTINGHAM

○ LINCOLN

L I N C O L N

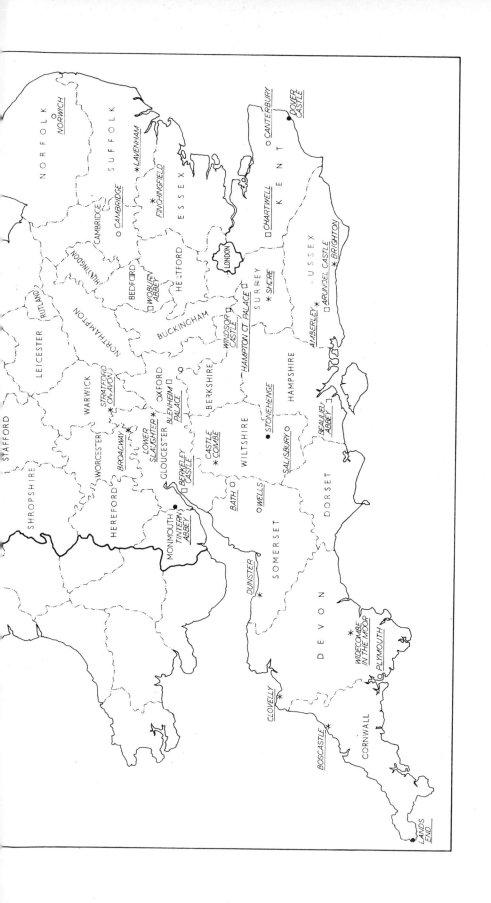

AUTHOR'S NOTE

The author is very conscious of the fact that he has done little more than skim the surface of the sights to be seen in this country, which in number and variety may be said to be out of all proportion to its relatively modest size. His book is designed to enable the visitor whose time is necessarily limited to see at least a representative selection of the Stately Homes, Castles, Cathedrals, Historic Buildings and Ancient Monuments, as well as the chief sights in London. His choice has largely been based on statistics which show those items most generally looked for by the visitor from overseas, especially from the United States of America and from Canada.

Any one item in the fifty selected could – as those who already know this country well appreciate – be matched by dozens, by scores, of others that equally merit inclusion. This is especially the case with the 'Show Towns and Villages'; the medieval half-timbering of Suffolk's Lavenham, for instance, can be matched in Herefordshire, Warwickshire, Cheshire and elsewhere; the golden limestone of Broadway and Lower Slaughter, typical of the Cotswolds, can be matched all along the oolitic limestone belt that stretches diagonally across England from the Dorset coast north-eastwards; the close-set harbour sites like Boscastle in Cornwall can be matched in coastal villages such as Staithes, in Yorkshire.

Briefly, this book can do little more than whet the appetite. Some of the titles listed at the beginning deal in ampler detail with the topographical scene; there are, too, countless books by other authors, many of them specialists in their individual subjects. It will be immediately evident that this sort of material is highly photogenic. Few travellers these days, at home or abroad, move far without their cameras, for the personal record is usually more satisfying than the bought photograph. Officially compiled guide-books are available at all the major sites included here, and countless others. The author's hope, however, is that he will have stimulated sufficient interest in the visitor for him to make his own photographic record and proceed to expand the outline information offered to him in the foregoing pages by studying in greater detail, and at his leisure, the subjects that particularly appeal to him. He will find that the choice and variety are inexhaustible.

Groombridge, Sussex.   G.H.

ACKNOWLEDGEMENTS

The author and publishers would like to express their thanks to the following for permission to reproduce illustrations supplied by them:

His Grace the Duke of Norfolk, 23 (above)

His Grace the Duke of Bedford, 41

Lord and Lady Montagu of Beaulieu, 25

Mr D. Hardley, 49

City of Bath Spa Department, 43

British Tourist Authority, 9, 11, 13, 15, 17, 19, 21, 23 (below), 27, 29, 31, 33, 35, 37, 39, 45, 47, 51, 53, 55, 57, 59, 61, 63, 65, 67, 69, 71, 73, 75, 77, 79, 81, 83, 85, 87, 89, 91, 93, 95, 97, 99, 101, 103, 105 and 107

INDEX BY COUNTIES